LOL

A LOAD OF
LAUGHS
AND
JOKES
for kids

LOL

A LOAD OF LAUGHS AND JOKES

for kids

Written and drawn by Craig Yoe

LITTLE SIMON

New York   London   Toronto   Sydney   New Delhi

LITTLE SIMON
An imprint of Simon & Schuster Children's Publishing Division
1230 Avenue of the Americas, New York, New York 10020
First Little Simon paperback edition August 2017
Copyright © 2017 by Craig Yoe
Portions of this material previously appeared in *The Mighty Big Book of Jokes*, *The Mighty Big Book of Riddles*, and *The Mighty Big Book of School Jokes* copyright © 2001, 2003 by Craig Yoe and in *Thanksgiving Jokes & Riddles*, *Valentine's Day Jokes & Riddles*, and *Christmas Jokes & Riddles* copyright © 2003 by Craig Yoe Studio, Inc.

For information about special discounts for bulk purchases, please contact Simon & Schuster Special Sales at 1-866-506-1949 or business@simonandschuster.com.
The Simon & Schuster Speakers Bureau can bring authors to your live event.
For more information or to book an event contact the Simon & Schuster Speakers Bureau at 1-866-248-3049 or visit our website at www.simonspeakers.com.
Designed by Hannah Frece
Manufactured in the United States of America 0717 FFG
2 4 6 8 10 9 7 5 3 1
This book has been cataloged with the Library of Congress.
ISBN 978-1-4814-7818-2 (pbk)
ISBN 978-1-4814-7819-9 (eBook)

To Griffin and Grace,
whom I deeply love and who
give me so many wonderful laughs!

Contents

This Place Is a Zoo!

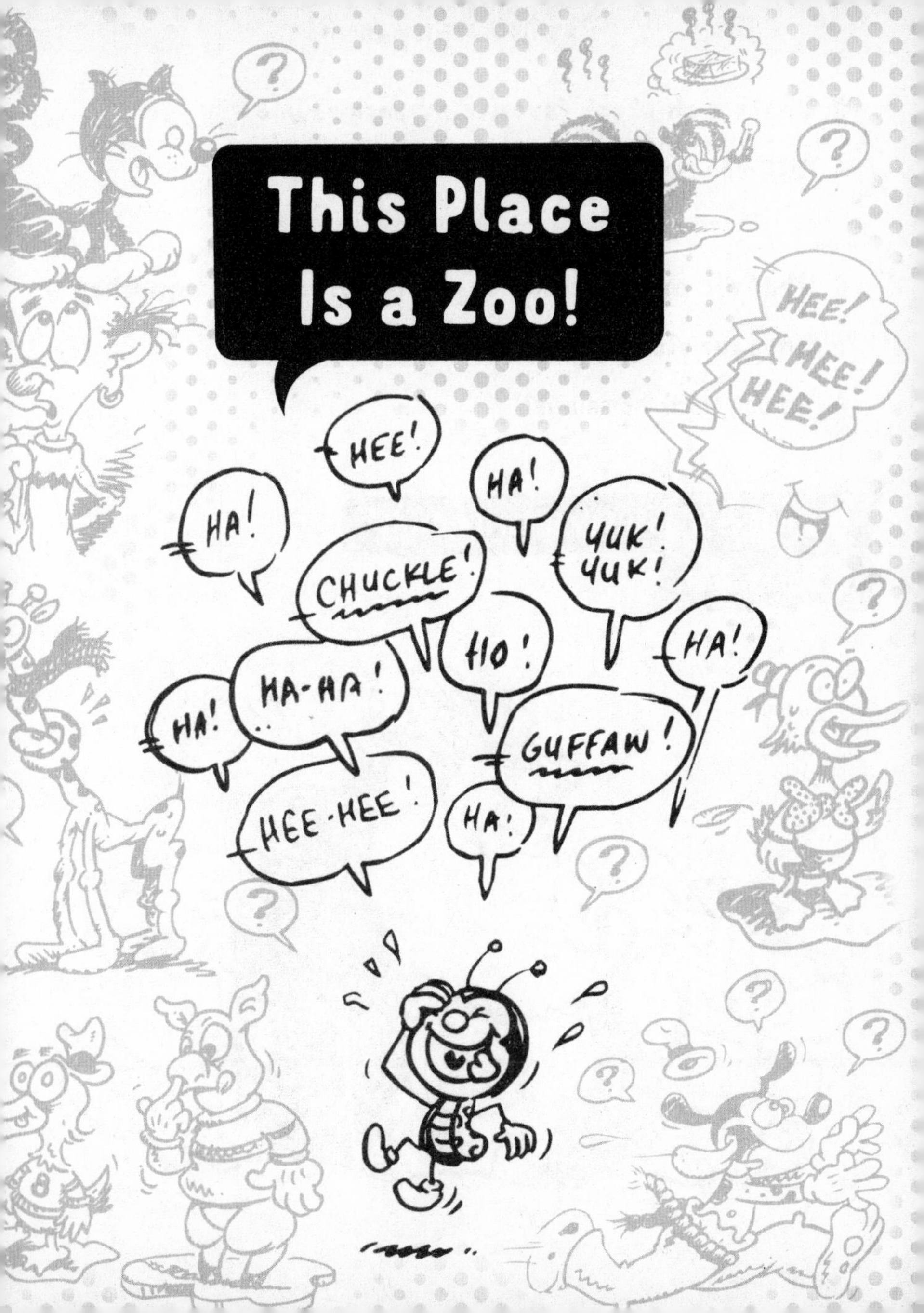

Q: What's a chicken's favorite nursery rhyme?

A: "Little Bo Peep-Peep!"

Q: What did one caveman say to the other caveman when a dinosaur stomped by?

A: "Do-you-think-he-saurus?"

Q: What is a gorilla's favorite drink?

A: Lemon-ape!

Q: How does a fairy tale about frogs end?

A: "They lived hoppily ever after!"

Q: Where do pigs keep their dirty clothes?

A: In the ham-per!

Q: Why do birds go to the library?

A: To look for book worms!

Q: Why shouldn't you tell a pig your secrets?

A: Because he'll squeal!

Q: What kind of truck does a frog drive?

A: A toad truck!

Q: Why did the turkey cross the road?

A: Because it was the chicken's day off!

Q: Why couldn't the dragon hold his job?

A: He kept getting fired!

Q: What kind of fish can you build things with?

A: A hammer-head shark!

Q: What do dogs wear when they play football?

A: Hel-mutts!

Q: What do you call a mouse that just took a shower?

A: Squeak-y clean!

Q: What does a squirrel with a sore tooth eat?

A: Ache-corns!

Q: What does a dog hate on his pizza?

A: Mozzarella fleas!

Q: What do you tell a selfish sheep?

A: It's not all about ewe!

Q: What does a cat do if he loses his tail?

A: He goes to a re-tail store!

Q: What do chickens do at Christmas?

A: Eggs-change gifts!

Q: Why did the sheep go to the doctor?

A: Because it was feeling baa-d!

Q: What does a cow put under her plate at dinner?

A: A place moo-t!

HA!

HA!

HA!

YOE!

Q: Did you hear that the pony can't talk?

A: Yes, it's a little hoarse!

Q: What does a vulture say before dinner?

A: "Let us prey!"

Q: What is a monkey's favorite cookie?

A: Chocolate chimp!

Q: What animals are the best swimmers?

A: Elephants—they always have their trunks on!

Q: Why did the cows get married?

A: Because they loved each udder!

Q: What did the goose say when it was stuck in traffic?

A: "Honk! Honk!"

Q: Where does a Tyrannosaurus rex go on vacation?

A: To the dino-shore!

Q: What did the ape write on his sweetheart's valentine?

A: "You're the gorilla my dreams!"

Q: Why are skunks good decision makers?

A: Because they have a lot of common scents!

Q: What is a dog's favorite food?

A: Anything on your plate!

Q: Why did the cow get a second job?

A: Because he needed to make more moo-lah!

Q: Why couldn't the pirate play cards with his parrot?

A: Because he was sitting on the deck!

Q: Why was the dog's nose flat?

A: Because he chased parked cars!

Q: What laughing animal is the most friendly?

A: A hi-ena!

Q: What did the goat say to his younger brother?

A: "Go away, kid, you bother me!"

Q: What is big and green and goes "gobble-gobble"?

A: Turkeysaurus rex!

Q: Why did the snake work at the gas station?

A: He was a windshield viper!

Q: Why shouldn't you insult a cat lover?

A: You'll hurt his felines!

Q: What did the duck family have after a shopping spree?

A: A lot of bills!

Q: What kind of swimming does a turkey do?

A: The turkey breast stroke!

Q: Why did the gorillas close their store?

A: Because they only got monkey business!

Q: What do rabbits say on Turkey Day?

A: "Hop-py Thanksgiving!"

Q: Why did the chicken sign up for band practice?

A: She wanted to use her drumsticks!

Q: What reptile is good to have around on moving day?

A: A box turtle!

Q: What kind of underwear do dogs wear?

A: Boxer shorts!

Q: What animal goes "Krab! Krab!"?

A: A dog barking backward!

Q: Where do cows and chickens go to get medicine?

A: The farm-acist!

Q: What message did the bat hear on the phone?

A: "Please hang upside down and try again!"

Q: What wild animals are the best dressed?

A: Tie-gers!

Q: Why did the turkey get in trouble?

A: He was using fowl language!

Q: What kind of dog can tell time?

A: A watch dog!

Q: When is it most unlucky to have a black cat cross your path?

A: When you're a mouse!

Q: What do you call a team of monkeys that wins a big game?

A: The chimp-ions!

Q: Why did the crab get coal for Christmas?

A: Because it was being shellfish!

Q: What position does a mule play on a football team?

A: Kicker!

Q: Where does a frog get his glasses?

A: At the hop-tometrist!

Q: Why do bears wear fur coats?

A: Because they would look silly in rain coats!

Q: What do you call a goose standing on its head?

A: Upside down!

Q: Why don't seagulls fly over a bay?

A: 'Cause then you'd have to call them bay-gulls!

Q: What's a skunk's favorite dessert?

A: Smell-o!

Q: Why did the dog run away from home?

A: Dog-gone if I know!

Q: What kind of gum does a whale chew?

A: Blubber gum!

Q: What do you get when you cross a big cat with a newspaper?

A: A head-lion!

Q: What did the sheep have on its thirteenth birthday?

A: A baa-mitzvah!

Q: Why did they have a funeral for the frog?

A: 'Cause it croaked!

Q: What do you call a really small mouse?

A: A pip squeak!

Q: What is a skunk's favorite snack?

A: Stench fries!

Q: What tree does a bear like to climb?

A: A fur tree!

Q: What do you get when you cross a monkey with dynamite?

A: Ba-booms!

Q: What do you use to wash a dog?

A: Sham-poodle!

Q: What did the cat say when she spilled her milk?

A: "Nobody's purr-fect!"

Q: Why did the radio station hire the canary?

A: He worked cheep!

Q: How do you know that's a baby snake?

A: It has a rattle!

Q: What time is it when a T. rex sits on your chair?

A: Time to get a new chair!

Q: Where do cows live in apartments?

A: In Moo York City!

Q: What has two humps and is found at the South Pole?

A: A lost camel!

Q: What does a chicken eat at the movies?

A: Peep-corn!

Q: What happened when the car was surrounded by two dogs?

A: It was double barked!

Q: Why was the lamb wandering around in the middle of the night?

A: Because she was sheep-walking!

Q: What kind of fish goes well with peanut butter?

A: Jelly fish, of course!

Q: Why did the duck wear a nose ring?

A: Because it fit the bill!

Q: What is a young snake's favorite school subject?

A: Hiss-tory!

Q: What cartoon dog would make a good spy?

A: Snoopy!

Q: What do you call a reindeer with an attitude problem?

A: Rude-olph!

Q: Why did the chicken cross the playground?

A: To get to the other slide!

Q: What is a cat's favorite toy?

A: A hair ball!

Q: Why do greyhounds like french fries so much?

A: Because they're fast food!

Q: I saw a lion sixteen feet long!

A: That's some lyin'!

Q: How do you know the frogs found the flies delicious?

A: They rated them "two tongues up"!

Q: What does an elephant call his father's sister?

A: Eleph-aunt!

Q: What hops up in the morning and crows?

A: A kanga-rooster!

Q: Why did the mother cat put stamps on her kittens?

A: Because she was delivering a litter!

Q: Guess what dog joined my football team?

A: A golden receiver!

Q: Where do cows post their messages at work?

A: On the bull-etin board!

Q: What caused the duck to get sick?

A: Beak-teria!

Q: What do you call an injured Tyrannosaurus rex?

A: A dino-sore!

Q: What class does a turkey wrestle in?

A: Feather weight!

Q: Why did the zoo get rid of the owl?

A: He didn't give a hoot!

Q: Why did the noisy dog get a ticket?

A: He didn't see the No Barking sign!

Q: How do you stop a scarf from slipping down a giraffe's neck?

A: Tie a knot in his neck!

Q: Why did the crow use her phone?

A: She wanted to caw her mother!

Q: What sound do porcupines make when they kiss?

A: "Smack! Ouch!"

Q: What do you get when you put too much mousse on your head?

A: Antlers!

Q: What part of your house is most like an animal?

A: The seal-ing!

Q: Why was the bull afraid of everything?

A: He was a cow-ard!

Q: Why did the bird go to the doctor?

A: He was feeling under the feather!

Q: Where is the best place to shop for a kitten?

A: A cat-alog!

Q: When does a duck say "oink"?

A: When she's learning a foreign language!

Q: Where does a squirrel write his class assignment?

A: In a nut-book!

Q: Are you sure there aren't any sharks around here?

A: Yes, the alligators scared them away!

Q: Where do baby cows eat lunch?

A: The calf-eteria!

Q: How do you know if a kitten has a broken leg?

A: Do a cat-scan!

Q: What is a dog's least favorite breath mint?

A: Tick tacs!

Q: What do you call an unexciting pig?

A: A boar!

Q: What do you call a boring dinosaur?

A: A dino-snore!

Q: Why don't hippos join the Boy Scouts?

A: They don't look good in green!

Q: What animals talk too much?

A: Yaks!

Q: Why did the national bird of the United States go to jail?

A: He was ill-eagle!

Q: What kind of cookies do birds like to bake?

A: Chocolate chirp cookies!

Q: Where do you take a snake that's been in an accident?

A: To the hiss-pital!

Q: What pet store product makes a cat go to sleep?

A: Cat-nap!

Q: What do you call it when a snake throws a tantrum?

A: A hiss-y fit!

Q: What musical instrument can you use to catch fish?

A: A clari-net!

Q: What kind of jokes do frogs tell?

A: Wise croaks!

Q: What kind of soup does a dog like?

A: Chicken poodle!

Q: Who brings presents to crows at Christmas?

A: Santa Claws!

Q: How do you call a dog with no legs?

A: Who cares? He won't come anyway!

Q: What food do rams like to eat?

A: Peanut butt-er!

Q: What's the least exciting animal at the North Pole?

A: A polar bore!

Q: What does a kangaroo eat at the movies?

A: Hop-corn!

Q: What do you call an elephant in a car seat?

A: Stuck!

Q: How does a dog walk through a wall?

A: With a door!

Q: What is a canary's favorite cereal?

A: With a door!

Q: How did the horse greet his next-door friend?

A: "Good morning, neigh-bor!"

Q: What do you call a bear in the snow?

A: A brrrrr!

Q: Which side of a dog has more hair?

A: The out-side!

Q: How does a bird see through a wall?

A: With a window!

Q: What do you call a reptile that doesn't like to take the stairs?

A: An alli-vator!

Q: What do you get when you cross a pony with a zipper?

A: A horse fly!

Q: What did the mother pig say to the piglet?

A: "Don't pork your nose!"

Q: What should you know before teaching a dog new tricks?

A: More than the dog!

Q: Why don't many canaries go to college?

A: Because they don't finish high school!

Q: Why do girl camels wear pink underwear?

A: To tell them apart from the boy camels!

Q: What do cats eat for dessert?

A: A chocolate mouse!

Q: How does a cat stop a video?

A: She clicks on paws!

Q: What do you call a bullfight?

A: A cattle battle!

Q: What's a toad's favorite part of a newspaper?

A: The warts pages!

Q: How does a shark win the race?

A: By crossing the fin-ish line!

Q: Why did the dragon become a snob?

A: Because the flame went to his head!

Q: What kind of animals can you buy with a dollar?

A: Four quarter horses!

Q: Where can you get a furry bandage?

A: From a first aid kit-ten!

Q: What do you say to the bunny on the day he's born?

A: "Hop-py birthday!"

Q: What game does a hen like to play?

A: Chick-ers!

Q: What do you call a crab that gives presents to good boys and girls?

A: Sandy Claws!

Q: How can you tell if there's an elephant in a peanut-butter jar?

A: You can't get the lid on!

Q: What do you call a group of giraffes going to a watering hole?

A: Necks in a line!

Q: Why did the kangaroo get mad at her kids?

A: Because they ate crackers in bed!

Q: Why did the boy get glasses for his pet porcupine?

A: Because he thought a cactus was his girlfriend!

Q: What does a chicken's computer screen say?

A: "Cluck here!"

Q: What's a dog's favorite snack?

A: Pup-corn!

Q: What did the boy snake give to the girl snake at the end of their date?

A: A good-night hiss!

Q: What fish plays in the orchestra?

A: A c-arp!

Q: What happened to the dog that swallowed a lot of clocks?

A: He got a lot of ticks!

Q: What did the beaver say to the tree?

A: "It was nice getting to gnaw you!"

Q: How does a toad end his e-mails?

A: "Hop to see you soon!"

Q: Why did the cow cross the road?

A: To get to the udder side!

Q: What has eight legs and barks?

A: Two dogs!

Q: When did the chicken cross the road?

A: At eggs-actly the right time!

Q: What did the mother turtle say to the shy baby turtle?

A: "You should come out of your shell!"

Q: What's a farm animal's favorite pasta?

A: Spa-goat-ti!

Q: How does one toad greet another?

A: "Wart's up?"

Q: Which animal is nothing like a hound dog?

A: Ewe ain't nothin' like a hound dog!

Q: Why don't cows take cruises?

A: Because they get moo-tion sickness!

Q: What is the lion-taming act at the circus?

A: The mane event!

Q: What's a chicken's favorite dessert?

A: A coop-cake!

Q: What has eight hoofs, three tails, and two horns?

A: A unicorn with spare parts!

Q: What did the dolphin say after the shark splashed him?

A: "You did that on porpoise!"

Q: **Why couldn't the hummingbird hum?**

A: Because he was hum-sick!

Q: **What do you call an Australian animal when it's being obnoxious?**

A: Kanga-rude!

Q: **What's the best day to adopt a cat?**

A: Cat-urday!

Q: Why do fish have scales and live in the water?

A: So you can tell them apart from a banana!

Q: What is a dog's philosophy?

A: The worst things in life are fleas!

Q: What do you get when you put an elephant and a peanut between two slices of bread?

A: A peanut and elephant sandwich!

Q: Why did the cow cross the road?

A: To go to the moo-vies!

Q: What does a cat have that nothing else has?

A: Kittens!

Q: What do you call a blind buck?

A: I have no-eye-deer!

Q: What does a cobra like to eat for dinner?

A: Snake 'n Bake!

Q: What's pink, cold, and very dangerous?

A: Shark-infested strawberry ice cream!

Q: How can you tell that a leopard just took a bath?

A: Because he's spotless!

Q: What animal shouldn't you invite to a parade?

A: A rain-deer!

Q: How do cows use a computer?

A: By moooooooving the mouse!

Q: What do you call it when your dog swallows your clock?

A: Alarming!

Q: Why does a cat make a great pet?

A: Because it's purr-fect!

Q: Why was the fish so unique?

A: He marched to the tuna his own drummer!

Q: Why shouldn't you trust big ferocious cats with manes?

A: Because they're always lion!

Q: What kind of fish drinks quickly?

A: A gulp-y!

Q: When do ducks have four feet?

A: When there are two ducks!

Q: Why did the monkey quit his job at the zoo?

A: It was driving him bananas!

Q: Why did Donner and Blitzen let Rudolph lead the reindeer team?

A: They didn't want to pass the buck!

Q: What do you get when you cross an elephant with a goldfish?

A: A fishbowl that needs to be cleaned daily!

Q: What's a pig's favorite music?

A: Hip-slop!

Q: How does a chimp open a banana?

A: With a mon-key!

Q: What do you call a cat in a red suit who rides in a sleigh?

A: Santa Paws!

Q: What kind of snake goes well with dessert?

A: A pie-thon!

Q: What do you call it when lots of apes get together?

A: A Kong-vention!

Q: Where do sheep get their hair cut?

A: The baa-baa shop!

Q: Why did the chicken get grounded?

A: He was using fowl language!

Q: What did the frog say when he ordered a hamburger?

A: "Does that come with flies?"

Q: Which of Noah's animals didn't come in pairs?

A: The worms . . . they came in apples!

Q: What is Mother Goose's favorite pasta?

A: Macaroni and geese!

Q: What does a cobra wear on his feet?

A: Snake-ers!

Q: What do you call a cow that gives chocolate milk?

A: An udder delight!

Q: Where does the chicken like to eat?

A: At a rooster-ant!

Q: What do ducks love to play?

A: Hide-and-beak!

Q: What part of a car looks most like an elephant?

A: The trunk!

Q: What is a crocodile hunter's favorite thing to drink?

A: Alli-gator-ade!

Q: What do you give a sheep you borrow money from?

A: An I. O. Ewe!

Q: Where does a squirrel like to shop?

A: At Wal-nut-mart!

Q: Why was the mama deer annoyed with the papa deer?

A: He was a buck-seat driver!

Q: What did the cat give the dog for his birthday?

A: Collie-flowers!

Q: What does a bear feel after a long winter's nap?

A: Den-ergetic!

Q: What does a Tyrannosaurus rex like to eat for breakfast?

A: An egg-o-saurus!

Q: What did the bee say through his apartment building intercom?

A: "I'll buzz you in!"

Q: What do you call a tired cow grazing in your backyard?

A: A yawn mooer!

Q: Why do spiders make good outfielders?

A: Because they can catch flies!

Q: What does a snake wear with a tuxedo?

A: A boa tie!

Q: How do you get your dog to eat underwater?

A: Feed him guppy chow!

Q: What happened after the leopard got hit on the head?

A: He saw spots!

Q: How do you know there's a T. rex under your bed?

A: Your head is touching the ceiling!

Q: Where does a worm like to vacation?

A: The Big Apple!

Q: What's a cow's favorite song?

A: "Jingle Bulls"!

Q: What did the tree say to the bird?

A: "Leaf me alone!"

Q: How does a cow like to travel?

A: In a mooooo-ving van!

Q: Why was the vet so busy?

A: It was raining cats and dogs!

Q: What do you get when you cross a bat with a dish?

A: A flying saucer!

Q: What is a rabbit's favorite kind of jewelry?

A: Anything made of fourteen-carrot gold!

Q: What do birds say on Halloween?

A: "Trick-or-tweet!"

Q: What do you get when you cross a porcupine with a balloon?

A: Pop!

Q: What does a crocodile call his GPS?

A: A navi-gator!

Q: What is more unusual than a singing dog?

A: A spelling bee!

Q: Why did the police dog say, "Quack quack"?

A: He was undercover!

Q: What did the leopard use to clean his coat?

A: Spot remover!

Q: Why was the poodle so happy?

A: He got a new leash on life!

Q: What do sparrows serve at parties?

A: Bird-day cakes!

Q: What has four legs, antlers, and little red shorts?

A: Mickey Moose!

Q: What song do Australian kids sing?

A: "Kangaroo-roo-roo Your Boat"!

Q: What do you say about a rabbit that turns into a monster?

A: "Hare today, goon tomorrow!"

Q: What is the best way to catch a fish with a computer?

A: Use the Inter-net!

Q: Why do you have to be careful when you cross from one state into another?

A: Because of the state lion!

Q: What eats peanuts and sings "The Star-Spangled Banner"?

A: A patriotic elephant!

HERE THERE

Q: Why did the boy bring scissors to school?

A: He wanted to cut the lunch line!

Q: Why did the watch get in trouble at school?

A: It was all wound up!

Q: What is a wizard's best school subject?

A: Spell-ing!

Q: Where do baby trees go to school?

A: A nursery!

Q: What did the students see on the desk in woodshop?

A: They saw dust!

Q: What do you call a ghost that goes to college?

A: A school spirit!

Q: Why did the frog study at night?

A: He was swamped with homework!

Q: What item of clothing always gets a good report card?

A: Smarty pants!

Q: What kind of tests would you get if Dracula was your teacher?

A: Blood tests!

Q: What time would it be if Godzilla came to school?

A: Time to run!

Q: Why didn't the zombie go to school?

A: He was feeling rotten!

Q: Why did the giant get into trouble at school?

A: Because he was telling tall tales!

Q: Where do you get extra credit for passing notes at school?

A: In music class!

Q: What does a farmer use in math class?

A: A cow-culator!

Q: Why can't you take an elephant to school?

A: Because he won't fit in your backpack!

Q: What is a witch's favorite school activity?

A: Spell-ing bees!

Q: What do you call a country that gives a lot of tests?

A: An exami-nation!

Q: What does an astronaut bring to the school cafeteria?

A: Launch money!

Q: Why did the vampire get in trouble in art class?

A: Because he drew blood!

Q: What tool is good at math?

A: Multi-pliers!

Q: What do you get when you mix up math and English?

A: Add-verbs!

Q: What was Frosty the Snowman's favorite year at school?

A: Frost grade!

Q: What is the most shocking story in the history books?

A: When Ben Franklin discovered electricity!

Q: Why did Frankenstein fail his math test?

A: He made too many t-errors!

Q: Why are calculators so reliable?

A: Because you can count on them!

Q: Why shouldn't you do homework on an empty stomach?

A: It's better to do it on a computer!

Q: How do donkeys get to school each day?

A: The mule bus!

Q: What did the straight-A student order in the school cafeteria?

A: An honor roll!

Q: What do you tell a librarian after you've left your books overnight in the rain?

A: Sorry my books are over-dew!

Q: What's the difference between HERE and THERE?

A: The letter *T*!

Q: What part of your eye goes to school?

A: The pupil!

Q: Where does Sunday come after Monday?

A: In the dictionary!

Q: What is a pirate's favorite subject in school?

A: Arrrrt!

Q: How do you fix a broken horn?

A: With a tuba glue!

Q: Why did the sheep go to the school nurse?

A: She wasn't feeling wool!

Q: What type of candy do you eat in the school yard?

A: Recess Pieces!

Q: Why did the math test go the school counselor?

A: Because it had a lot of problems!

Q: What did the monkey get on his finals?

A: All apes!

Q: Which geometry figure is like a runaway parrot?

A: A polygon!

Q: What did the class clown order in the school cafeteria?

A: Hilari-tea!

Q: Why do soccer players do well in school?

A: They're always using their heads!

Q: When the runner came in second place, what did the coach tell him to eat?

A: Ketchup!

Q: What should you do when your tongue is all red?

A: Bring it back to the library!

Q: Where did the superhero go during school vacation?

A: Cape Cod!

Q: What time do you have to get out of class to go to the dentist?

A: Tooth-hurty!

Q: What do you call a group of aliens who play instruments as they walk?

A: A school Martian band!

Q: What is the quietest school team you can join?

A: The bowling team—you can hear a pin drop!

Q: What did the lunch lady do when she was angry?

A: She gave everyone a pizza her mind!

Q: Why is the letter A like a flower?

A: Because a bee comes after it!

Q: Why did the dog do well in school?

A: Because he was the teacher's pet!

Q: What does a pig use to take notes?

A: A pig pen!

Q: What did the mechanic give to his prom date?

A: A car-sage!

Q: Why did the captain of the track team do so well in English?

A: He was a speed reader!

Q: What did the art teacher use to paint the river?

A: Water-colors!

Q: What kind of test does a dog take?

A: A pup quiz!

Q: What was the school color for a school with a cat mascot?

A: Purr-ple!

Q: Why did the ladder fail its history test?

A: It got the answers rung!

Q: What is a cow's favorite class?

A: Moo-sic!

Q: What is the librarian's name?

A: Rita Book!

Q: What insect gets the best grades in English?

A: The book worm!

Q: Which kind of sandwiches do temporary teachers eat?

A: Subs!

Q: What does the French teacher say when she feeds her dog?

A: "Bone appétit!"

Q: What do you learn from a teacher who teaches health and math classes?

A: Lung division!

Q: What sport did the Easter Bunny play in school?

A: Basket-ball!

Q: What happened when the monster acted up in class?

A: The teacher called his mummy!

Q: Why did the student get kicked out of music class?

A: He kept getting in treble!

Q: What did the bug say to her friend?

A: "Will you help me with my moth homework?"

Q: What do you call the line in the school cafeteria?

A: The chew-chew train!

Q: Why was the school nurse's canary sick?

A: Flu!

Q: What did the dog order in the school cafeteria?

A: Pooch-ed eggs!

Q: What time does school start in a chicken coop?

A: Eight o'cluck!

Q: Where does the honor student keep his goldfish?

A: In a think tank!

Q: What did the goat order in the school cafeteria?

A: Butt-ered toast!

Q: What is the painting teacher's name?

A: Art N. Crafts!

Q: Where do cows hang their artwork at school?

A: On the bull-etin board!

Q: What do music teachers like to watch on TV?

A: Car-tunes!

Q: Why did the dog go to the school nurse?

A: It was feeling arf-ful!

Q: Why was the basketball team upset with its team picture?

A: It was a foul shot!

Q: Which school has the shortest basketball team?

A: Junior Height School!

Q: What does an astronomer get on his paper when he does well?

A: Gold stars!

Q: Why did the duck get sent to the principal's office?

A: He was a wise-quacker!

Q: What color likes books?

A: Red!

Q: Why did the teacher show the class the elephant at the zoo?

A: The lion was busy!

Q: Why did the lightning bug go to the school nurse?

A: It had glowing pains!

Q: Why can't you take your dog to school?

A: It's a no barking zone!

Q: Why was the math book sad?

A: It had a lot of problems!

Q: What does a skunk order when the cafeteria serves spaghetti?

A: A side of stench bread!

Q: What letter is the opposite of out?

A: *N*!

Q: What does Dr. Jekyll like to play at recess?

A: Hyde-and-seek!

Q: What kind of cheese does the lunch lady feed her dog?

A: Mutts-arella!

Q: Why did the principal buy a canary instead of a parrot?

A: It was cheep-er!

Q: Why did the teacher go to the eye doctor?

A: She was having trouble with her pupils!

Q: Why did the math teacher win the argument with the English teacher?

A: Because fractions speak louder than words!

Q: What's written above the door of a dog obedience school?

A: The school mutt-o!

Q: What do you say when the lunch lady gives you a hot dog?

A: "Franks a lot!"

Q: Why did the student go to English class?

A: Because the class wouldn't come to him!

Q: Where does the average student go on vacation?

A: C World!

Q: What's a pig's favorite school subject?

A: Sty-ence!

Q: Who first used fractions?

A: Louis the 1/16!

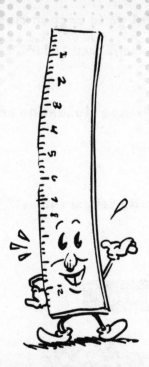

Q: What does a king use to measure things?

A: A ruler!

Q: Why did the ghost get thrown out of class?

A: He spooked out of turn!

Q: Why did the teacher put cat litter in the classroom?

A: For the teacher's pet!

Q: Why are anesthesiologists good at math?

A: Because of all the numb-ers!

Q: What do you get when you cross a police officer with the lunch lady?

A: Captain Cook!

Q: Where did the geography teacher take his dog for vacation?

A: Collie-fornia!

Q: What did the student say about the arithmetic exam?

A: "It was sum test!"

Q: What can't you have until it's taken?

A: Your school picture!

Q: What will happen if you don't pass your history exam?

A: History will repeat itself!

Q: What kind of pet does a school nurse have?

A: A first aid kit-ten!

Q: Why should you bring a ladder to music class?

A: So you can sing higher!

Q: Where does a music teacher order her lunch?

A: At the count-er!

Q: Where do they hold weird school plays?

A: In the odd-itorium!

Q: What's the most stressful part of school?

A: De-tension!

Q: Why did the clock get in trouble in class?

A: Because it tocked too much!

Q: Why did the teacher start dating the janitor?

A: He swept her off her feet!

Q: What did the school counselor say when the student was looking for the way out?

A: "Which way did you come in?"

Q: Why did the big cat get an F on his report card?

A: Because he was a cheetah!

Q: Why did the art teacher have his puppy swallow a clock?

A: He wanted a watch dog!

Q: What letter is always surprised?

A: O!

Q: What happened when the wizard acted up in school?

A: He got ex-spelled!

Q: Where did Sir Lancelot earn his diploma?

A: In knight school!

Q: Why did the egg get thrown out of class?

A: Because he kept telling yolks!

Q: What did the health teacher's cat say when it got attacked by a dog?

A: "Me-ouch!"

Q: Why did the clown go to the school nurse?

A: He felt funny!

Q: Why did the teacher have bad manners?

A: She had no class!

Q: Why did the captain of the basketball team eat cookies with milk?

A: He liked to dunk!

Q: Which school team do cows play on?

A: The base-bull team!

Q: Why did the teacher wear sunglasses?

A: Because his students were very bright!

Q: What did the school nurse say to the monster after checking his eyesight?

A: "You have 20/20/20/20 vision!"

Q: What does a bee ride to school?

A: The school buzz!

Q: Why did the frog make the school baseball team?

A: He was good at catching flies!

Q: Which number isn't hungry?

A: Eight!

Q: What do penguins ride to school?

A: Their b-ice-cycles!

Q: Why did the cows go to prom together?

A: Because they loved each udder!

Q: What is the laziest thing in the school cafeteria?

A: The nap-kins!

Q: What did the student say when asked to bring a pocket calculator to school?

A: "I already know how many pockets I have!"

Q: What did the monkey wear in home economics class?

A: An ape-ron!

Q: Why is a hot dog smart?

A: She made the honor roll!

Q: Why did the banana get voted prom queen?

A: She had a lot of a-peel!

Q: Where do dishonest people go to study?

A: The lie-brary!

Q: What part of a desk is an art teacher's favorite?

A: The draw-ers!

Q: Who runs the school and is also your best friend?

A: The princi-pal!

Q: Where do clocks keep their books at school?

A: In their clockers!

Q: What should you use to blow your nose in the cafeteria?

A: Dish-ues!

Q: Why did the kangaroo go to the school nurse?

A: He wanted to find out if he needed a hop-eration!

Q: What do you do when a pig chokes in the school cafeteria?

A: The ham-lich maneuver!

Q: What do you call a school gymnasium with poor lighting?

A: A dim gym!

Q: What did the science teacher say when asked why birds fly south?

A: "Well, it's too far to walk!"

Q: What do turtles give in surprise quizzes?

A: Snappy answers!

Q: Why did the boy get an F on his report on dolphins?

A: He didn't do it on porpoise!

Q: What is Hercules's favorite subject?

A: Mythmatics class!

Q: **When do you eat grapes while at school?**

A: At bunch time!

Q: **Which class is a bored person's favorite?**

A: Sigh-ence!

Q: **Where do birds keep their books at school?**

A: In their flockers!

Q: **What monster is the best at arithmetic?**

A: Count Dracula!

Q: **What do pigs do after school?**

A: Ham-work!

Q: **What's louder than a cheerleader?**

A: Two cheerleaders!

Q: **When is the gym teacher's dog most likely to run away?**

A: When the door is open!

Q: How do you spell mousetrap?

A: C-A-T!

Q: What kind of books do they read in Dallas?

A: Tex-books!

Q: Where was the principal when the school lights went out?

A: In the dark!

Q: What did the pizza say to the teacher?

A: Nothing. Pizzas don't talk!

Q: What is a monkey's favorite thing at recess?

A: The jungle gym!

Q: What word is always spelled right?

A: Right!

Q: What color should a cheerleader's uniform be?

A: Yell-ow!

Q: Which teacher always has a cold?

A: The mu-sick teacher!

Q: Why did the kid eat his homework?

A: Because he didn't have a dog!

Q: What did the art teacher say during the duel?

A: "Draw!"

Q: Which teacher sends the most notes home?

A: The music teacher!

Q: Why was the insect excited when he saw his report card?

A: Because he got killer Bs!

Q: How do you know a dinosaur is in your locker?

A: You can't shut the door!

Q: Why did the golfer do so well in school?

A: He was the teacher's putt!

Q: How does the principal get to school?

A: On the school boss!

Q: Which pet plays in the marching band?

A: A trum-pet!

Q: Why did the apple go to the school nurse?

A: It felt rotten!

Q: What is the physical education teacher's name?

A: Jim Nasium!

Q: What kind of tree is good at math?

A: A geome-tree!

Q: Why did the charge card turn in more homework?

A: It wanted extra credit!

Q: What did the teacher's dog say to the flea?

A: "Go away! You're bugging me!"

Q: What letter can you sail on?

A: C!

Q: What did the bat learn in kindergarten?

A: The alpha-bat!

Q: Who invented airplanes that couldn't fly?

A: The Wrong brothers!

Q: How did the rabbit react when he failed the test?

A: He got hopping mad!

Q: What is a math teacher's favorite dessert?

A: Pi!

Q: What do you call a skeleton who doesn't do her homework?

A: Lazy bones!

Q: Why was the pig thrown out of the school football game?

A: He played dirty!

Q: Why was the monkey sent to the principal's office?

A: She was a bad-boon!

Q: What do you call someone who has a straight-A report card in their pocket?

A: Smarty pants!

Q: What sound does a principal's phone make?

A: A school ring!

Q: Why did the chicken stay home from school?

A: He had people pox!

Q: What kind of pet would the science teacher have if he crossed a pig with a gerbil?

A: A ham-ster!

Q: What kind of school did Princess Belle go to?

A: Beauty school!

Q: How do hornets get to school?

A: They take the school buzz!

Q: What does a window use to take notes?

A: A pen-sill!

Q: What is the school band's favorite month?

A: March!

Q: What instrument does a turkey play in the marching band?

A: Drums, because he has the drumsticks!

Q: What should you use to find your way if you get lost in math class?

A: A compass!

Q: What instrument would a roof play in the school band?

A: Gui-tar!

Q: Which teacher needs the most substitutes?

A: The mu-sick teacher!

Q: Which letter can you see with?

A: The letter I!

Q: Where do you learn to swim?

A: In diver's ed!

Q: What do you call someone who wears a uniform, carries pom-poms, and loves books?

A: A cheer-reader!

Q: What kind of people does the school librarian dislike?

A: Book-keepers!

Q: Why did the members of the tennis team get jobs in the cafeteria?

A: They were good at serving!

Q: What did President Lincoln learn in school?

A: The Abe, B, C's!

Q: What is a teacher's favorite candy?

A: Chalk-olate!

Q: Where can you find the largest diamond?

A: In a school baseball field!

Q: What do you call a student with four heads?

A: A quadruple pupil!

YOE!

Q: What did the art teacher say when the students asked her if painting is difficult?

A: "No, it's easel!"

Q: Why did the boy swallow the dollar bill his mother gave him?

A: She told him it was lunch money!

Q: What did a monkey bring the teacher on the first day of school?

A: Ape-ples!

Q: Why did the zombie lose the track race at school?

A: He was dead last!

Q: What has two hundred feet and sings?

A: The school choir!

Q: What does spaghetti play in gym class?

A: Meat-ball!

Q: Who is an English teacher's favorite relative?

A: His grammar!

Q: What team do lazy students join?

A: The rest-ling team!

Q: What instrument would a dog play in the school band?

A: Trom-bone!

Q: Why was the book scared?

A: It was spineless!

Q: What did the ghost wear to school?

A: Boo jeans!

Q: Why is a school cafeteria worker like a train?

A: She says, "Chew, chew"!

Q: Where does an insect write his homework assignments?

A: In a gnat-book!

Q: What does a music teacher use to call home?

A: A saxo-phone!

Q: What is a tailor's favorite subject?

A: Sew-cial studies!

Q: Why did the refrigerator try out for the track team?

A: It was always running!

Q: Why did everyone in class have to get bandages?

A: They went on a school trip!

Q: What drink is found in the alphabet?

A: Tea!

Q: Why did the small bucket go to see the school nurse?

A: It was looking a little pail!

Q: What is the longest word in the English language?

A: Smiles—there's a mile in between the first and last letter!

Q: What did the librarian say when the vegetables walked into the library?

A: "Peas whisper!"

Q: What do you get when you cross a vampire with a teacher?

A: A blood test!

Q: Why are bunnies so good at math?

A: Because they multiply so quickly!

Q: What is the biggest punctuation mark?

A: The fifty-yard dash!

Q: Where do you sit in math class?

A: At the multiplication table!

Q: What is a shopper's favorite class?

A: Buy-ology!

Q: Why did the pig get the lead in the school play?

A: He was a big ham!

Q: What subject is a rodent's favorite?

A: Lite-rat-ure!

Q: What is a computer's favorite musical instrument?

A: The keyboard!

Q: Where do cows go on class trips?

A: To the moo-seum!

Q: What country do they serve in the school cafeteria?

A: Chile!

Q: What other country do they serve in the school cafeteria?

A: Turkey!

Q: What did the ocean say when summer vacation was over and all the kids were leaving?

A: Nothing, it just waved!

Q: Why did the broom get in trouble?

A: He was caught sweeping in class!

Q: What's a school librarian's favorite food?

A: Ma-shhh-ed potatoes!

Q: What do you get when you cross a barber and a librarian?

A: A barbarian!

Q: Why couldn't the piano teacher open the door to his classroom?

A: Because all the keys were inside!

Q: Why did the piece of corn join the school band?

A: It had an ear for music!

Q: Why did the pair of scissors become a school bus driver?

A: It knew a lot of short cuts!

Q: Why did the math teacher open his classroom window?

A: He needed some air-ithmetic!

Q: What did the student say when the teacher asked her why she was late for class?

A: "I came early for next period!"

Q: Why did the coffee cup get detention?

A: It was latte for class!

Q: Where did the geology teacher take her class on a school trip?

A: To a rock concert!

Q: Why didn't the skeleton go to prom?

A: He had no body to go with!

Q: Why is a book like a watermelon?

A: Because on the inside it's red!

Q: What do kangaroos love to play at recess?

A: Hopscotch!

Q: What did the salt say to the pepper in the cafeteria?

A: "What's shakin'?"

Q: Why did Rose do so well in school?

A: She was a budding genius!

Q: Why did the student drop his computer class?

A: He was key-bored!

Q: What animal is found in the alphabet?

A: Ewe!

Q: What does a ghoul order at a restaurant?

A: Choking potpie!

Q: What wears a cape, has fangs, and is found underwater?

A: A clam-pire!

Q: What do ghosts have on their bicycle wheels?

A: Spooks!

Q: Why was the Invisible Man always so nervous?

A: He was afraid of his own shadow!

Q: Who did the witch give candy to on Valentine's Day?

A: Her sweet-wart!

Q: What does a mummy wear on Halloween?

A: A cos-tomb!

Q: Which monster has a really positive attitude?

A: Fran-can-stein!

Q: What did the mommy monster say to the baby monster at dinner?

A: "Quit goblin your food!"

Q: Who did the zombie take to the prom?

A: His ghoul-friend!

Q: How does a monster count to twelve?

A: On its toes!

Q: How do scary monsters say good-bye to each other?

A: "Fear well!"

Q: What did the ghoul tell his mother when she bought him new clothes?

A: "I wouldn't be caught dead in those!"

Q: What do you call a zombie who appears in a lot of movies?

A: A mon-star!

Q: What's scarier than a vampire?

A: Two vampires!

Q: Why do skeletons always drink milk?

A: So they can have strong bones!

Q: What kind of job does Dracula have?

A: He's an ac-count-ant!

Q: Why did the watch get thrown out of class?

A: It was caught making faces!

Q: What did the cannibals say to their neighbors?

A: "We'd love to have you for dinner!"

Q: What is the mummy's favorite school subject?

A: English de-composition!

Q: What game do monsters like to play?

A: Truth or scare!

Q: What does a ghost use when he plays the guitar?

A: Sheet music!

Q: Why did the vampire use mouthwash?

A: So he wouldn't have bat breath!

Q: What's furry, has claws, and always comes in twos?

A: A pair-wolf!

Q: What do ghosts read?

A: Booo-ks!

Q: What is the scariest time for a chicken?

A: When there's a fowl moon!

Q: What kind of sandwiches does a mummy eat for lunch?

A: Wraps!

Q: Where do zombies get their messages?

A: In their eek-mail!

Q: Why couldn't the teacher grade the Invisible Man's homework?

A: He wrote it in invisible ink!

Q: What does a spirit eat for breakfast?

A: Ghost toasties!

Q: What did Frankenstein feel when he met the Bride of Frankenstein?

A: Love at first fright!

Q: How did the vampire get on the baseball team?

A: He got to be the bat boy!

Q: Where do you go when you want to buy a zombie?

A: To a mon-store!

Q: What happened to the ghoul when he was in junior high school?

A: He grew a foot!

Q: What did the zombie say on the way out the door?

A: "It's been nice gnawing you!"

Q: What's furry, has claws, and never wears any clothes?

A: A bare-wolf!

Q: What does a monster yell before hitting a golf ball?

A: "Fear!"

Q: What does a monster do with his mouthwash?

A: He gargoyles!

Q: Where does a ghost go to learn how to cut hair?

A: Booo-ty school!

Q: What do skeletons say before going on a trip?

A: "Bone voyage!"

Q: What does Dracula wear around his neck to keep warm?

A: A scare-f!

Q: What do you call a big green monster that drools a lot?

A: Franken-slime!

Q: Why did the ghoul want to leave summer camp?

A: He missed his mummy!

Q: What do you call a car driven by Dracula?

A: A blood mobile!

Q: What do you get when you cross a vampire with a bell?

A: A ding-bat!

Q: Why couldn't the dog become a vampire?

A: His bark was worse than his bite!

Q: What did the zombie like in math class?

A: Die-vision!

Q: What does a ghost order in an Italian restaurant?

A: Spook-ghetti!

Q: What did the Cyclops teacher say in the teachers' lounge?

A: "I only have one pupil this year!"

Q: How did the Invisible Man's mother know when he was lying?

A: She could see right through him!

Q: Why did the ghost blow his nose?

A: Because it was full of booo-gers!

Q: What is big, green, and plays a lot of tricks?

A: Prank-enstein!

Q: Where do werewolves go after their wedding?

A: On their honey-full-moon!

Q: What do you tell Dracula when his ego gets out of control?

A: "It's not all about Drac-you-la!"

Q: What wears a cape, has fangs, and tastes good on toast?

A: A jam-pire!

Q: What is as big as Godzilla but weighs nothing?

A: His shadow!

Q: What monster is black and yellow and buzzes?

A: A zom-bee!

Q: What do vampires eat at baseball games?

A: Fang-furters!

Q: What did the mummy professor say at the end of class?

A: "That wraps it up!"

Q: What does a skeleton say before dinner?

A: "Bone appetit!"

Q: What do ghosts wear in the snow?

A: Booo-ts!

Q: What kind of key should you use to get into a haunted house?

A: A skeleton key!

Q: What do you say when you meet a four-headed monster?

A: "Hello! Hello! Hello! Hello!"

Q: What does a ghost wear when he's reading?

A: Spook-tacles!

Q: What is big and green and is worth ten cents?

A: Franken-dime!

Q: What do you get if you cross a mummy with a bottle of perfume?

A: Whatever it is, don't smell it!

Q: What wears a cape, has fangs, and has lots of wool?

A: A lamb-pire!

Q: Why don't demons go to the gym?

A: They hate exorcising!

Q: Why did Dracula become an artist?

A: He liked to draw blood!

Q: Why did the Bride of Frankenstein go to the gym?

A: To keep her ghoulish figure!

Q: What does a sorceress order at a restaurant?

A: A sand-witch!

Q: What kind of songs do ghosts like?

A: Haunting melodies!

Q: Why did the vampire like computers so much?

A: Because of all the bytes!

Q: What is big and green and eats a lot of hot dogs?

A: Franks-enstein!

Q: Where do ghosts go on vacation?

A: Lake Eerie!

Q: Who never shows up for work?

A: The Invisible Man!

Q: What happened when the two twenty-foot giants met?

A: It was love at first height!

Q: What does a monster musician sing to warm up his voice?

A: "Dracu-la-la-la!"

Q: Why did the ghost become a cheerleader?

A: Because she had a lot of school spirit!

Q: Where did the Bride of Frankenstein go to school?

A: An all-ghouls school!

Q: Why didn't the vampire have many friends?

A: He was a pain in the neck!

Q: Where do most ghouls live?

A: On a dead-end street!

Q: What did the ghost do for extra credit in school?

A: He became a hall moan-itor!

Q: What wears a cape, has fangs, and comes from a pig?

A: A ham-pire!

Q: What's little, gray, and visited by ghosts?

A: A haunted mouse!

Q: What do ghosts watch on TV?

A: Horror booo-vies!

Q: What does Dracula never order at a restaurant?

A: A stake!

Q: How do monsters get to school?

A: On the ghoul bus!

Q: What does Frankenstein order for dessert at a restaurant?

A: Ice scream!

Q: What is a ghost's favorite fruit?

A: Boo-berries!

Q: When are monsters the silliest?

A: When there's a fool moon!

Q: What did Dracula learn in first grade?

A: The alpha-bat!

Q: Which werewolf dresses in red and brings presents to kids?

A: Santa Claws!

Q: What does a ghost make when he gets a test answer wrong?

A: A booo-booo!

Q: What ghost always has a broken arm?

A: Cast-per!

Q: What's green and scary and bounces?

A: Frankenstein on a pogo stick!

Q: What kinds of wizards make pasta?

A: Saucer-ers!

Q: What is a vampire's favorite holiday?

A: Fangs-giving!

Q: What's big and green and smells really bad?

A: Stank-enstein!

Q: Why did the vampire get thrown out of class?

A: He was being very bat!

Q: What does a mummy order at a restaurant?

A: Tomb-ato soup!

Q: What's furry, has claws, and always gives his things to others?

A: A share-wolf!

Q: Why did the monster stop going out with the Invisible Man?

A: She wasn't seeing enough of him!

Q: What is Dracula's favorite fruit?

A: Neck-tarines!

Q: What does Frankenstein eat for breakfast?

A: Dreaded wheat!

Q: What instrument does a skeleton play?

A: A trom-bone!

Q: What did the doctor say when the monster had a baby?

A: "It's a ghoul!"

Q: What do you call a monster who cleans floors?

A: A mop-ster!

Q: What has fangs and 102 floors?

A: The Vampire State Building!

Q: What's a ghost's favorite game?

A: Hide-and-eek!

Q: What does a monster chew?

A: Booo-ble gum!

Q: What does a monster eat at a baseball game?

A: A Hallo-weiner!

Q: What did the ghost give his girlfriend?

A: A boo-quet of flowers!

Q: What is Dracula's favorite ice cream flavor?

A: Vein-illa!

Q: What is big, green, and lives in an aquarium?

A: Tank-enstein!

Q: Why do ghosts love libraries?

A: Because they love booo-ks!

Q: Who signs the Invisible Man's report cards?

A: His trans-parents!

Q: What does the witch have on her phone?

A: Cauldron waiting!

Q: What is a monster's favorite drink?

A: Ghoul-Aid!

Q: What do werewolves say when they greet each other?

A: "Hi, howl are you?"

Q: What street do zombies live on?

A: A dead-end street!

Q: Who did Dracula ask to his high school prom?

A: The head cheer-bleeder!

Q: What did the monster do to improve his grades?

A: Extra crud-it!

Q: Why did Frankenstein get in trouble at school?

A: He was caught in the ghouls' bathroom!

Q: What did the skeleton principal say to the bad student?

A: "I have a bone to pick with you!"

Q: Why did the ghoul fail his exam?

A: He made a grave mistake!

Q: What has fangs, horns, and wears a cape?

A: A ram-pire!

Q: What kind of dog does Dracula have?

A: A bloodhound!

Q: What do you get when you give Frankenstein some snow?

A: A snowball fright!

Q: What do you call a duck that turns into a vampire?

A: Quack-ula!

Q: Why was the skeleton late coming home?

A: He had to stay after skull!

Q: How do monsters like their coffee?

A: With scream and sugar!

Q: What did Frankenstein do when he got a funny valentine?

A: He laughed his head off!

Q: What is Dracula's favorite sport?

A: Bat-minton!

Q: What is silky, has sleeves, and is visited by ghosts?

A: A haunted blouse!

Q: Why are witches such good shoppers?

A: They like to hag-gle!

Q: What's furry, has claws, and is really hard to find?

A: A rare-wolf!

Q: What does a zombie order in a restaurant?

A: Corn on the corpse!

Q: Where does Dracula get his money?

A: From the blood bank!

Q: Why do mummies never get married?

A: Because they have cold feet!

Q: Where do monsters go to learn about the future?

A: To a fear-tune teller!

Q: Why was Dracula always looking in the mirror?

A: He was a little vein!

Q: What should you do if you see a werewolf?

A: Run as fur away as you can!

Q: What did the tuna sand-witch say on the stove?

A: "I'm melting!"

Q: Why did the vampire go to the insane asylum?

A: He went batty!

Q: What is furry, has claws, and is always taking chances?

A: A dare-wolf!

Q: Why is Frankenstein green?

A: Because he's on a boat and got seasick!

Q: When do most monsters trip while they're walking?

A: When there's a fall moon!

Q: When should you have a werewolf as a pet?

A: When he's house-trained!

Q: What does a ghost bride throw at the end of her wedding?

A: The booo-quet!

Q: What do you call a monster that looks at you without blinking?

A: A mon-stare!

Q: Why did the monster dance so badly on his date?

A: He had six left feet!

Q: What sign does a monster put up when he goes to the lake?

A: Goon fishing!

Q: When is the best time for a monster to get in touch with his feelings?

A: When there's a feel moon!

Q: Where do vampires live?

A: At the end of a Dracul-de-sac!

Q: What was the pretty monster voted in the class poll?

A: Most boo-tiful!

Q: Why was the skeleton always afraid?

A: Because he had no guts!

Q: What is Dracula's favorite piece of clothing?

A: A neck-tie!

Q: What does a ghost do as soon as he gets in a car?

A: Fastens his sheet belt!

Q: Who wrote these monster jokes?

A: A ghostwriter!

Q: What side of a werewolf is the furriest?

A: The outside!

Q: Where do most vampires live?

A: Cape Cod!

Q: What did Casper do after high school?

A: He joined the Ghost Guard!

Q: Why did Dracula go to the chiropractor?

A: He had a pain in the neck!

Q: What do you call a zombie with a lot of kids?

A: A mom-ster!

Q: What's green, lives in the woods, and has antlers?

A: Frankenstein's moose-ter!

Q: Who makes the scariest screams?

A: Moan-sters!

Q: What's married and visited by ghosts?

A: A haunted spouse!

Q: What did the mother witch say to the daughter witch when she was in trouble?

A: "Go to your broom!"

Q: Where does Frankenstein fly out of when he goes on a trip?

A: The scare-port!

Q: What is a sea monster's favorite food?

A: Fish-and-ships!

Q: What kind of clock is big and green, has fangs, and yells at you to wake up?

A: An alarming clock!

Q: What creature puts money under Dracula's pillow at night?

A: The fang fairy!

Q: Why do comedians love it when werewolves come to their shows?

A: Because they howl with laughter!

Q: What wears a cape, has fangs, and is blue?

A: A vampire holding his breath!

Q: What monster always has a runny nose?

A: The Boogie Man!

Q: Why did the witch do poorly in school?

A: Because she couldn't spell!

Q: Why did the ghost like waking up early?

A: Because he was a moaning person!

Q: What is Dracula's favorite school subject?

A: Hearse-tory!

Q: What ghost do you eat for breakfast?

A: Casper the Friendly Toast!

Q: What did Frankenstein do when he got in trouble?

A: He bolted!

Q: How do you know when Dracula has a cold?

A: He'll be coffin!

Q: Why did the monster stay home from school?

A: He had scare-let fever!

Q: What monster spills food on his clothes?

A: Franken-stains!

Q: What's furry, has claws, and has big floppy ears?

A: A hare-wolf!

Q: What does Dracula use to make pancakes?

A: Bat-ter!

Q: Why did the monster fail his driver's test?

A: He made too many t-errors!

Q: How did the ghost win the football game?

A: He kicked a field ghoul!

Q: What do you get when you cross Dracula with a snowman?

A: Frostbite!

Q: What's furry, has claws, and has games and rides?

A: A fair-wolf!

Q: What is Frankenstein's favorite sport?

A: Boo-sketball!

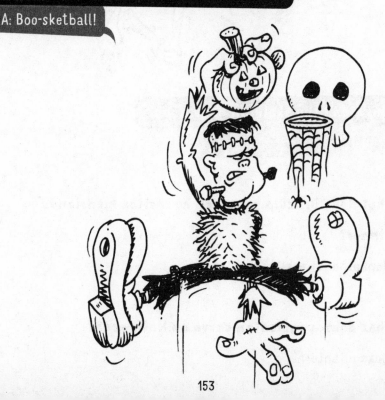

Q: Why didn't the skeleton have a job?

A: Because he was a lazybones!

Q: What does Dracula say when he invites his friends to dinner?

A: "Wanna go for a bite?"

Q: What does a comedian carve on Halloween?

A: A joke-o'-lantern!

Q: What did Dracula say after the dinner party?

A: "Fang you very much!"

Q: What do you call a ghost that just bought a new house?

A: A home moaner!

Q: What does a vampire drink on Halloween?

A: Dra-cola!

Q: Why did Dracula take a keyboarding class?

A: So he could learn to blood type!

Q: What position did the ghost play on the soccer team?

A: Ghoulie!

Q: What kind of music do ghosts like the most?

A: Rhythm and boos!

Q: Where does Dracula go for vacation?

A: Cape Town!

Q: Why didn't the skeleton cross the road?

A: He didn't have the guts!

Q: Why does Dracula love computers?

A: Because of all the mega-bites!

Q: What does a ghost drink in the morning?

A: Coff-eek!

Q: Why do witches like to ride their brooms?

A: Vacuum cleaners are too heavy!

Q: What do you call Frankenstein when he's angry?

A: Frank-incensed!

Q: What do you get when you combine Dracula and winter?

A: Frostbite!

Q: When is the Invisible Man visible?

A: When he has a kid, he's a-parent!

Q: Where does a girl ghost go to get ready for a date?

A: To the scare-dresser!

Q: What do you get when you cross Dracula with a goose?

A: Count down!

Q: Where do monsters go to school?

A: Goon-iversities!

Q: What is a monster's favorite ice cream flavor?

A: Shock-olate!

Q: What does the Abominable Snowman say when he's down and out?

A: "The snow must go on!"

Q: What happened when Dracula and Wolverine had a fight?

A: They fought tooth and nail!

Q: What do you call zombies with a lot of kids?

A: Mom-sters!

Q: What do you get when you combine Dracula with an artist?

A: Drawing blood!

Q: What kind of comedy routine does a witch perform?

A: Broom shtick!

Q: Why does Dracula keep his mouth shut?

A: Because silence is ghoul-den!

Q: What is Dr. Jekyll's favorite game?

A: Hyde-and-seek!

Q: What do you call a sorceress's tic?

A: A witch twitch!

Q: What does a rotting mummy smell like?

A: You don't want to know—it Sphinx!

Q: What kind of computer does a Cyclops use?

A: The Eye-Mac!

Q: How do you start a letter to a mummy?

A: Tomb it may concern!

Q: What does a zombie like on his potatoes?

A: Grave-y!

Q: What color hair do most witches have?

A: Brew-nette!

Q: What did the monster install on his computer?

A: A scream saver!

Q: What does the ghost say when he makes a mistake?

A: "I made a boo-boo!"

Q: Where does the king of skeletons sit?

A: A bone throne!

Q: What happened when Frankenstein drank a glass of milk?

A: He made the milk shake!

Q: Why did the Invisible Man go insane?

A: Out of sight, out of mind!

Q: What has three horns and dribbles a ball?

A: A three-horned ball dribbler!

Q: Why did the witch fly along the seashore?

A: She wanted a broom with a view!

Q: Why didn't the skeleton do her homework?

A: She was a lazybones!

Q: What happened to the extremely hairy man who walked into the woods?

A: Bigfoot took pictures of him!

Q: What is the best way to talk to a monster?

A: Long distance!

Q: What did the Bride of Frankenstein put on her face?

A: Cover Ghoul makeup!

Q: What do ghosts wear in the rain?

A: Boo-ts!

Q: What did Dracula say after biting his first victim?

A: "Necks, please!"

Q: Where did the monster keep his extra pair of arms?

A: In a hand-bag!

Q: What did the mommy monster say to her son?

A: "Quit picking your noses!"

Q: In what key did the monster play his song?

A: The skeleton key!

Q: What do you get when you combine a Scottish legend with your dad's wife?

A: The Loch Ness Mom-ster!

Q: What do you get when you cross Godzilla with a bottle of perfume?

A: I don't know, but I'm not going to smell it!

Q: Why did the ghost get in trouble at the dinner table?

A: He was goblin up his food!

Q: What's so unusual about the Invisible Man?

A: Well, you don't see one every day!

Q: What do you call Dracula's accent?

A: A fang twang!

Q: If a man named Cy was cloned, what would the new Cy be called?

A: Cy-clone!

Q: Why did the witch buy a forklift?

A: To raise her spirits!

Q: What do you call an owl's ghost?

A: A boo-whoo!

Q: Why did Godzilla wear purple boxer shorts?

A: Because his pink ones were in the laundry!

Q: What do movie-star monsters say?

A: "Boo-ray for Hollywood!"

Q: What do you call a wacky baker?

A: A dough-nut!

Q: What is the saddest thing to put on pumpkin pie?

A: Weeping cream!

Q: What fruit is yellow and blue?

A: An unhappy banana!

Q: What kind of fruit did Noah take on the ark?

A: Pears!

Q: What kind of berry always seems sad?

A: A blue-berry!

Q: What kind of berry always has a sore throat?

A: A rasp-berry!

Q: What kind of berry makes a loud honking noise?

A: A goose-berry!

Q: What kind of berry needs help drinking from a glass?

A: A straw-berry!

Q: What's a police officer's favorite food?

A: Corn on the cop!

Q: What did the cheerleader say to the sushi?

A: "Raw! Raw! Raw!"

Q: Why did the egg become a comedian?

A: Because it knew a lot of yolks!

Q: What did the cereal say to the juice at breakfast?

A: It proposed a toast!

Q: Which frozen treat can you ride?

A: A Pop-cycle!

Q: Why did the prune lose the NASCAR race?

A: It made too many pit stops!

Q: What is a rapper's favorite food?

A: Yo-gurt!

Q: What doesn't a police officer like on toast?

A: Traffic jam!

Q: Why didn't the banana go to work?

A: It had a splitting headache!

Q: What vegetable brings you good fortune?

A: Gar-luck!

Q: What topping does a razor like on strawberry shortcake?

A: Shaving cream!

Q: What's the best way to keep ice cream from melting?

A: Eat it!

Q: What's worse than finding a worm in an apple?

A: Finding half a worm!

Q: What did one hamburger patty say to the other hamburger patty?

A: "We're on a roll!"

Q: What vegetable didn't a sailor want on his boat?

A: A leek!

Q: What did the orange call his beloved tangerine?

A: "My darling Clementine!"

Q: What do prisoners eat in jail?

A: Cell-ery!

Q: Why did the doughnut maker go bankrupt?

A: He couldn't get out of the hole!

Q: What's a choirmaster's favorite lunch?

A: A hum sandwich!

Q: Why do chickens lay eggs?

A: So they don't break!

Q: What do you call it when a bean goes swimming?

A: A bean dip!

Q: What did one egg say to the other egg?

A: "Keep your sunny side up!"

Q: Why did the apple go to the doctor?

A: Because he felt rotten to the core!

Q: What is a bathtub's favorite dessert?

A: A cake of soap!

Q: What does a house like to drink?

A: Roof beer!

Q: What food is pink, cold, and very dangerous?

A: Scorpion-infested strawberry ice cream!

Q: What is a golfer's favorite drink?

A: Iced tee!

Q: How do you fix broken spaghetti noodles?

A: With a little tomato paste!

Q: Why did the basketball player snack on cookies and milk?

A: Because he liked to dunk!

Q: What happened when the potato got pulled over by the police?

A: He got a spud-ding ticket!

Q: What did one piece of bread say to the other on Valentine's Day?

A: "I loaf you!"

Q: What did the banana say to the pea?

A: "Let's split!"

Q: What is a practical joker's favorite food?

A: Prank-furters!

Q: What did the hamburger say to the bottle while running down the street?

A: "Catch up!"

Q: What girl likes oysters?

A: Pearl!

Q: What boy loves pickles?

A: Dill-on!

Q: What girl has a real sweet tooth?

A: Candy!

Q: What is most like half an apple?

A: The other half!

Q: Why do lazy people bake bread?

A: Because they like to loaf!

Q: What vegetable can see?

A: Gar-look!

Q: Why is the spaghetti smarter than the meatball?

A: Because it uses its noodle!

Q: What kind of food always has something nice to say?

A: Complimentary peanuts!

Q: What is an actor's favorite ice cream?

A: Star-berry!

Q: How do you get chocolate milk?

A: You milk chocolates!

Q: What kind of soup weighs 2,000 pounds?

A: One-ton soup!

Q: Why is a baseball game like a pancake?

A: Its success depends on the batter!

Q: Where did they put the burger when he was arrested?

A: In the patty wagon!

Q: Where did the police take the cabbage that broke the law?

A: To a court of slaw!

Q: Who is a vegetable's favorite musical composer?

A: Beet-hoven!

Q: What does a little dog order on his pizza?

A: Pup-peroni!

Q: What does a goat like on a baked potato?

A: Butt-er!

Q: Which restaurant serves pies that you wear on your head?

A: Pizza Hat!

Q: How can you start the day with a smile?

A: Eat grin-ola!

Q: Why do people keep the refrigerator door closed?

A: So you can't see the salad dressing!

Q: What kind of sandwich does a whale like to eat for lunch?

A: Peanut butter and jellyfish!

Q: Why was the cocoa never on time?

A: Because it was choco-late!

Q: What is a truck driver's favorite food?

A: Mack-aroni and cheese!

Q: What is the coolest part of a salad?

A: The rad-ishes!

Q: What does Frosty the Snowman eat on Thanksgiving?

A: Cold slaw!

Q: What do you call a vegetable that's old and rotten?

A: Aspara-gross!

Q: When do ice cream and hot fudge like to get together?

A: On Sundaes!

Q: What do polar bears like to eat in their salads?

A: Cucumbrrrrrs!

Q: What happened when the two bakers met?

A: It was loaf at first sight!

Q: What fruit comes in a pod?

A: Pea-ches!

Q: How did the paramedic revive the vegetable?

A: He used C-PEA-R!

Q: Where do you throw apple cores after you've eaten the apple?

A: In a used core lot!

Q: What do you call a dance where you get to know the butchers?

A: A meat ball!

Q: What fruit do you download on your smartphone?

A: An app-le!

Q: What's black and white and yellow and green?

A: A taxi-cabbage!

Q: Why do potatoes make good detectives?

A: Because they keep their eyes peeled!

Q: What's red, grows on trees, and has purple wheels?

A: An apple—I lied about the wheels!

Q: In what room do you make porridge?

A: In a mush-room!

Q: Why did the baker quit his job?

A: He kneaded more dough!

Q: What does a pickle say when he wants to play Crazy Eights?

A: "Dill me in!"

Q: What do you get when you combine vegetables with superheroes?

A: Beetman and Radish!

Q: What's green and goes up and down?

A: A pickle on a seesaw!

Q: Which vegetable is most appealing?

A: Cute-cumbers!

Q: What do you call a nonskid pancake?

A: A waffle!

Q: What did the celery say to the radish at the dance?

A: "Turnip the music!"

Q: What's a hero sandwich?

A: The opposite of a chicken sandwich!

Q: What city eats the most cherries?

A: Pitts-burgh!

Q: What's round and green and wins beauty contests?

A: Pretty peas!

Q: What's a weight lifter's favorite snack?

A: Bench fries!

Q: What is a space critter's favorite candy bar?

A: A Milky Way!

Q: What cookies should you eat on a rowboat?

A: Oar-eos!

Q: When is a Chinese restaurant successful?

A: When it makes a fortune, cookie!

Q: What vegetable do you put on ice cream?

A: Gar-lick!

Q: What do you get when you eat too much breakfast?

A: Waf-full!

Q: What food does a dentist like?

A: Pizz-ahhhh!

Q: What comes from another planet and tastes good in hot chocolate?

A: Martian-mallows!

Q: Why did the cashew go see the psychiatrist?

A: He was feeling nutty!

Q: What is always broken before it is eaten?

A: An egg!

Q: Why did the cornstalk go to the mall?

A: To get its ear pierced!

Q: What do you call an Englishman who eats fifty sandwiches a day?

A: Sir Lunch-a-lot!

Q: What does a baby corn kernel call its father?

A: Popcorn!

Q: **What vegetable can be found on a door?**

A: Gar-lock!

Q: **What do you call a pumpkin that works at the beach?**

A: A life gourd!

Q: **What do viruses like to eat?**

A: Chicken pox pie!

Q: **What's a frog's favorite soft drink?**

A: Croak-a-cola!

Q: **Why did the lazy person get a job at the bakery?**

A: He liked to loaf around!

Q: **How did the cook invent macaroni?**

A: He used his noodle!

Q: **How does a fire-eater like his steaks?**

A: Flame broiled!

Q: What is the messiest sport?

A: Ice cream bowl-ing!

Q: What football team eats corn for one dollar?

A: The buck-an-ears!

Q: What's the best advice you can give peanut butter?

A: "Stick to your gums!"

Q: What does a cat like to have for dessert?

A: Mice cream!

Q: What do polar bears like to eat?

A: Burrrrrrr-itos!

Q: What do you call cheese that's tastier than all the others?

A: A better cheddar!

Q: What does a head of hair eat for breakfast?

A: Dandruff flakes!

Q: What do cats like to eat?

A: Purrrrr-itos!

Q: What do you call a cheese that is sad?

A: Blue cheese!

Q: What do you call a joke about bread?

A: A bread shtick!

Q: Where do elderly eggs live?

A: In an old yolks' home!

Q: What do you get when you cross a windstorm with a vegetable?

A: Aspara-gust!

Q: What did the Pilgrims eat during their voyage to America?

A: Fish-and-ships!

Q: What does a boxer hate to eat for lunch?

A: A knuckle sandwich!

Q: What do you call a really juicy watermelon?

A: A wetter-melon!

Q: What is a guitar's favorite vegetable?

A: String beans!

Q: How does a flea make a cake?

A: From scratch!

Q: What is a plumber's favorite fruit?

A: A water-melon!

Q: What's green and sour and bounces?

A: A pickle on a trampoline!

Q: What do rich people eat on their birthday?

A: Twenty-four-carrot cake!

Q: What is a locksmith's favorite fruit?

A: Key-wi!

Q: What meal is easily broken?

A: Break-fast!

Q: What is a scarecrow's favorite fruit?

A: Straw-berries!

Q: What is green and has 102 floors?

A: The Empire State Pickle!

Q: What's purple and fixes your pipes?

A: A plum-ber!

Q: What do you say when you think the cheese is yummy?

A: "This cheese tastes gouda!"

Q: Why doesn't a golfer want pumpkin pie on Thanksgiving?

A: He doesn't want to have a slice!

Q: What is the best pizza joke?

A: A cheesy one!

Q: What is orange and then purple, orange and then purple, orange and then purple?

A: A carrot wrestling with a grape!

Q: Why did the sailor use a straw?

A: So he wouldn't fall into the drink!

Q: What did the butcher say to the bologna?

A: "Nice to meat you!"

Q: What is the result when one strawberry meets another strawberry?

A: A strawberry shake!

Q: Which breakfast cereal is used to protect castles?

A: Moat-meal!

Q: What kind of ice cream does a sailor like?

A: Boat-er pecan!

Q: What kind of soup does Mickey Mouse's girlfriend like?

A: Minnie-strone!

Q: What's a tailor's favorite drink?

A: Sew-da!

Q: What state can you bake with?

A: Flour-ida!

Q: What vegetable did the Pilgrim get lost in?

A: Maize!

Q: What did the music teacher dip her vegetables in?

A: Hum-mus!

Q: Why was the orange absent from school?

A: She wasn't peeling well!

Q: What do radiators eat at a Mexican restaurant?

A: Fa-heat-as!

Q: What does a dog eat at the movies?

A: Pup-corn!

Q: What kind of keys does a baker use to start his car?

A: Coo-keys!

Q: If your shoes were a fruit, what fruit would they be?

A: A pear!

Q: What is a repairman's favorite snack?

A: Wrench fries!

Q: What do you call spaghetti that makes fun of people?

A: Mock-aroni!

Q: What country eats the most fried food?

A: Greece!

Q: Why did the lemon take a nap?

A: She ran out of juice!

Q: What's sour and has two wheels?

A: A motorpickle!

Q: What is orange and goes "slam, slam, slam, slam"?

A: A four-door carrot!

Q: What happened when the strawberries got into a car accident?

A: They caused a traffic jam!

Q: What did the critic say about the new outer space restaurant?

A: "The food was good, but there was no atmosphere!"

Q: If you have twenty apples in one hand and seventeen in the other, what do you have?

A: Either really big hands or really small apples!

Q: What do you do when you hear a good peanut butter joke?

A: Spread it!

Q: What do vegetables use to send overnight packages?

A: United Parsley Service!

Q: What do you call popcorn kernels that don't pop?

A: Flop-corn!

Q: What two things can you not eat for breakfast?

A: Lunch and dinner!

Q: What shouldn't you drink when you have a cold?

A: Cough-ee!

Q: When do you eat almonds?

A: For a mid-nut snack!

Q: What's green and lights up?

A: An electric pickle!

Q: What does a golfer like on Thanksgiving?

A: Par-tatoes!

Q: Which ran furthest—the hamburger or the hot dog?

A: The frank further!

Q: How many cranberries grow on a bush?

A: All of them!

Q: What does a diamond like to eat?

A: Twenty-four carrots!

Q: What does a cat like to eat?

A: Purr-tatoes!

Q: What does a blackboard like to eat?

A: Chalk-olate!

Q: What's the nicest vegetable at the dinner table?

A: The sweet potato!

Q: What did one raw vegetable say to the other raw vegetable?

A: "Let's go for a dip!"

Q: Why are pumpkin pies so obnoxious?

A: Because they're very crusty!

Q: What do you get when you cross Clark Kent with noodles and broth?

A: Soup-erman!

Q: What is a singer's favorite food?

A: A hum-burger!

Q: What does a two-thousand-pound elephant eat on Thanksgiving?

A: Ton-key!

Q: Why do bakers make pumpkin pie?

A: They knead more dough!

Q: What does a cactus eat after dinner?

A: Desert!

Q: What does a hippie put on his potatoes?

A: Groovy!

Q: What food always eats too fast?

A: The cram-berries!

Q: What does a golfer like to eat for dessert?

A: Chocolate putt-ing!

Q: Why was the butter successful?

A: He was on a roll!

Q: What do you call potatoes that fall on the floor?

A: Smashed potatoes!

Q: What do you eat a very small piece of pie with?

A: Sliver-ware!

Q: Why did the vegetables have to leave the dinner table?

A: They were all fresh!

Q: What is ice cream's favorite part of a parade?

A: All the floats!

Q: What vegetable can you use to tie your shoes?

A: String beans!

Q: What does a road eat on Thanksgiving?

A: Tar-key!

Q: What is a choirmaster's favorite food?

A: Hymn-burgers!

Q: What does Santa Claus eat at a Mexican restaurant?

A: Chimney-changas!

Q: What dessert do police officers like to eat?

A: Cop-cakes!

Q: What's the best thing to have on top of a piece of pumpkin pie?

A: Another piece of pumpkin pie!

Q: Why are potatoes good at finding things?

A: They keep their eyes peeled!

Q: Why did the grape kiss the banana?

A: Because it had a-peel!

Q: What's a turtle's favorite drink?

A: Snap-ple!

Q: What is the most dangerous thing to order in a school cafeteria?

A: Piranha-infested tomato soup!

Q: What position does an banana play on the baseball field?

A: Ripe field!

Q: What kind of cereal does a math teacher eat?

A: Alge-bran!

Q: Why should you wear a sweater to a Tex-Mex restaurant?

A: In case they serve chili!

Q: What's the weirdest thing you'll see in the school cafeteria?

A: An apple turn over!

Q: What do you call a Thanksgiving dish that studies hard for a test?

A: Cram-berry!

Q: Why did the lunch lady cook with so many onions?

A: She found them a-peel-ing!

Q: Why did the meatball walk up the road?

A: It wanted to get to the fork!

Q: What is the nicest thing at dinner?

A: The sweet peas!

Q: What cafeteria food makes you throw up?

A: Spew-ghetti!

Q: What did the lunch lady use to make her dog cookies?

A: Collie flour!

Q: What did the frog say when he got a hamburger?

A: "Can I get flies with that?"

Q: What does a skunk order at a fast-food restaurant?

A: Stench fries!

Q: What happens when a hot dog does well in school?

A: It makes the honor roll!

Q: What happened when the omelet acted up in school?

A: It got eggs-pelled!

Q: Why did the wizard eat alphabet soup?

A: She wanted to cast a spell!

Q: **When is a student's homework like an undercooked steak?**

A: When it's rarely done!

Q: **What does a thirsty kid order when the cafeteria serves hamburgers?**

A: Quench fries!

Q: **What did the kid look like after finishing his desserts?**

A: Pie-eyed!

Q: What does a foot eat when the school cafeteria serves Mexican food?

A: Burri-toes!

Q: Which Thanksgiving beverage is sad?

A: Apple sigh-der!

Q: What do they serve in the cafeteria at sorcery school?

A: Sand-witches!

Q: What is the coolest food in the cafeteria?

A: The rad-ishes!

Q: Why did the banana get voted class president?

A: She had a lot of a-peel!

Q: When does red mean go and green mean stop?

A: When you're eating a watermelon!

Q: What does a burglar like in his soup?

A: A safe cracker!

Q: What drink is found in the alphabet?

A: Iced tea!

Q: Why didn't anyone like the potatoes?

A: Because they were duds!

Q: What does spaghetti play in gym class?

A: Meatball!

Q: What is the best thing to do on a lazy day?

A: Go to the school cafeteria and watch the meat loaf!

Q: What did the Pilgrims use to bake cakes?

A: May-flour!

Q: Why did the music teacher play piano?

A: Because you can't tune a fish!

Q: What does a janitor eat at the movies?

A: Mop-corn!

Q: What did the salt say to the pepper?

A: "What's shakin'!"

Q: What type of candy is the loudest?

A: Yell-y beans!

Q: What do you think of the bread?

A: "I loaf it!"

Q: **What did the librarian say when the vegetables walked into the library?**

A: "Peas be quiet!"

Q: **On what day do they serve fish in the cafeteria?**

A: On fry-day!

Q: **Where do you go after eating beans in the school cafeteria?**

A: Fart class!

P.F.P.T!

Q: What should you do when the cafeteria serves blueberries?

A: Try to cheer them up!

Q: What vegetable is found in the alphabet?

A: Pea!

Q: What do you call an unlucky olive?

A: Pit-iful!

Q: What does the lunch lady like on her hot dog?

A: Cat-sup!

Q: Where should you put the corn and carrots on Thanksgiving?

A: On the vege-table!

Q: Why was the peach so happy?

A: Because it felt warm and fuzzy!

Q: Why did the student stop eating pizza?

A: His heath teacher told him he needed to eat square meals!

Q: What pasta do you wear with a suit?

A: Bowtie!

Q: What do you get when you combine a soda with a bike?

A: A Pop-cycle!

Q: What kind of ice cream did the snake order?

A: Asp-berry!

Q: What's a pen's favorite drink?

A: Ink lemonade!

Q: What kind of candy does a dad like?

A: Lolli-pop!

Q: What did the ice cream cone get after graduation?

A: A dip-loma!

Q: What is a history teacher's favorite fruit?

A: Dates!

Q: On what day do they serve fries in the cafeteria?

A: On fry-day!

Q: Why did the corn go to the doctor?

A: It had an ear ache!

Q: What does Dracula like to eat?

A: Neck-tarines!

Q: What do you eat at the beach?

A: Sand-wiches!

Q: What does an English teacher order in the cafeteria?

A: An Edgar Allen Poe-tato!

Q: What state did the geography teacher say is a pig's favorite?

A: New Pork!

Q: Why did one eye think the other eye farted?

A: Because something smelled between them!

Q: Why is hot faster than cold?

A: You can catch a cold!

Q: What does a fisherman do in a fire?

A: Stop, drop, and reel!

Q: What color loves boating?

A: Oar-ange!

Q: What did the composer do to improve his tennis game?

A: He worked on his Bach-stroke!

Q: What is the difference between a shiny dime and a dirty quarter?

A: Fifteen cents!

Q: Why do scientists look for things over and over?

A: Because they re-search everything!

Q: What song makes you laugh?

A: "Tickle, Tickle, Little Star"!

Q: Why did the swimmer call his barber before the big race?

A: To shave a couple of seconds off his time!

Q: Why shouldn't you mow the lawn with a smile?

A: It's better to use a lawn mower!

Q: What did the bee say to the rose?

A: "You're my best bud!"

Q: What would Old MacDonald say if he were a rapper?

A: "E-I-E-I-YO!"

Q: What starts with a *T*, is filled with *T*, and ends with a *T*?

A: A teapot!

Q: How many feet are in a yard?

A: That depends on how many people are standing in it!

Q: How did you get that flat tire?

A: There was a fork in the road!

Q: What do you call a funny undershirt?

A: A tee-hee shirt!

Q: What kind of insect do you swallow to relieve a cold?

A: A decongest-ant!

Q: What do computers and test dummies have in common?

A: They both like to crash!

Q: What is at the end of the road?

A: The letter *D*!

Q: Why did the musician quit his job?

A: Things hit a sour note!

Q: Why can't your head be twelve inches long?

A: Because then it would be a foot!

Q: What can speak every language but never went to school?

A: An echo!

Q: Which New York Yankee wears the biggest cap?

A: The one with the biggest head!

Q: What's green, has four wheels, and hauls cars?

A: A toad truck!

Q: Why do chimney sweeps like their jobs?

A: It soots them!

Q: What is a bee's favorite haircut?

A: A buzz cut!

Q: What do you call a baby stable?

A: A new-barn!

Q: Why was the living room arrested?

A: Because it was in possession of an armed chair!

Q: Why did Rosemary take a shortcut?

A: To save thyme!

Q: What do hunters use to style their hair?

A: Moose!

Q: What note does a buzzing insect play?

A: Bee-sharp!

Q: What do you call a bad haircut?

A: A hair scare!

Q: Why is the nose in the middle of the face?

A: Because it's the scent-er!

Q: What does a genie use to blow his nose?

A: Wish-ues!

Q: Where can you store food in a forest?

A: In the pan-tree!

Q: What does a sailor take to prevent sickness?

A: Vitamin sea!

Q: Where does January come after February?

A: In the dictionary!

Q: What tool does a carpenter need to build a playground?

A: A see-saw!

Q: When you look into the mirror in the morning, which continent do you see?

A: You're-up!

Q: Why are worms always depressed?

A: They don't have a funny bone in their body!

Q: What did the painting say to the police?

A: "I've been framed!"

Q: What does the joke writer wear under his pants?

A: Pun-derwear!

Q: What did the place mat say to the silverware?

A: "Dinner's on me tonight!"

Q: What did the volcano say to the valley?

A: "I lava you!"

Q: Why did King Kong climb the Empire State Building?

A: The elevator was out of order!

Q: What does a king do after visiting the bathroom?

A: A royal flush!

Q: What does Popeye put in his car?

A: Olive oil!

Q: Why did the clown work in the clock factory?

A: He liked making faces!

Q: What do you say to an electrician?

A: "Thanks a watt!"

Q: What kind of noodles can catch a cold?

A: Mac and sneeze!

Q: Why do hummingbirds hum?

A: They forget the words to the songs!

Q: Where does Clark Kent buy his food?

A: At the Super market!

Q: What do you call a snowman in the spring?

A: A puddle!

Q: What kind of shirt can you drink?

A: A tea-shirt!

Q: What did the baseball mitt say to the catcher?

A: Nothing. Baseball mitts don't talk!

Q: What roof is always wet?

A: The roof of your mouth!

Q: What do you always overlook?

A: Your nose!

Q: How do you make a piano laugh?

A: Tickle its ivories!

Q: What do basketball players and babies have in common?

A: They both dribble!

Q: Why did the bee get sent to the principal's office?

A: Because of his bad bee-hive-ior!

Q: What is a baby's favorite search engine?

A: Goo-Google!

Q: What does a race-car driver get at a hotel?

A: Vroom service!

Q: What did the dad armpit say to the kid armpit?

A: "Respect your odors!"

Q: What's a robot's favorite snack?

A: Nuts and bolts!

Q: **What part of a television is most like a window?**

A: The screen!

Q: **What did the target say after the archer missed him?**

A: "I had an arrow escape!"

Q: **Where does the anteater go to get his prescriptions filled?**

A: To the ant farm-acy!

Q: **What did the garbage collector's mother say?**

A: "Quit talking trash!"

Q: **When do you need to change a baby's diaper?**

A: In the wee-wee hours of the morning!

Q: **What kind of exercise can you do on a boat?**

A: A-row-bics!

Q: What is a gorilla's favorite fruit?

A: An ape-ricot!

Q: How did the seamstress feel today?

A: Sew-sew!

Q: What kind of flower do you cook with?

A: A pan-sy!

Q: What bug is good at math?

A: An account-ant!

Q: What kind of computer does a pole vaulter use?

A: A leap top!

Q: Why didn't the teddy bear want dessert?

A: He was stuffed!

Q: What does a zookeeper wear when cooking?

A: An ape-ron!

Q: What does a baseball player keep on his doorstep?

A: A welcome mitt!

Q: What's the best piece of gym equipment for weight loss?

A: A trampo-lean!

Q: What kind of transportation do you use to get to the bathroom?

A: The tub-way!

Q: How does a cartoonist get to work?

A: In a car-toon!

Q: What did one snowflake say to the other snowflake?

A: "There's snow business like snow business!"

Q: What kind of jewelry is a soccer player's favorite?

A: Goal-d!

Q: What kind of music did the Pilgrims dance to?

A: Plymouth Rock!

Q: How does a car run without an engine?

A: You just put a hill under it!

Q: What does a king do in an emergency?

A: Stop, drop, and rule!

Q: What's more incredible than a singing dog?

A: A spelling bee!

Q: What smells the most in a garbage dump?

A: The nose!

Q: Why did the photographer quit his job?

A: He snapped!

Q: What do apes like to ride in?

A: Hot-air baboons!

Q: What did one tire say to the other tire?

A: "Quit skidding around!"

Q: Where do dishonest people go to read?

A: The lie-brary!

Q: What kind of furniture do ants like?

A: Ant-iques!

Q: Where does Snow White keep her clothes?

A: In the seven drawers!

Q: On what kind of bed do you hit your head?

A: A bonk bed!

Q: What does a salesperson make phone calls on?

A: A sell phone!

Q: What did the boat do when it was feeling sick?

A: It went to the dock-tor!

Q: What did Spider-Man do when he borrowed the Batmobile?

A: He took it for a spin!

Q: What did the mommy credit card say to the kid credit card?

A: "Swipe your nose!"

Q: What does a mountain use to play baseball?

A: A sum-mitt!

Q: What does a carpenter do when he works in the hot sun?

A: He sweats nails!

Q: What did one tree say to the other tree at the end of the day?

A: "I gotta leaf!"

Q: What does a jigsaw puzzle do after a bad experience?

A: It tries to pick up the pieces!

Q: What was the poor locksmith always looking for?

A: The key to success!

Q: Why doesn't Tarzan's monkey like to play games?

A: Because cheetahs never win!

Q: What kind of book does a bug like to read?

A: Rom-ants novels!

Q: Why did the toilet go to the doctor?

A: It was feeling flushed!

Q: Why did the zookeeper wear glasses?

A: Because he had spots in front of his eyes!

Q: What does a robot do when he's late?

A: He bolts out the door!

Q: Why did the firefighter leave his job?

A: He wanted to quit before he got fired!

Q: What's the best way to pass a test in music class?

A: Study your notes!

Q: What do you call a deck of cards with 4,529 cards?

A: A big deal!

Q: Why did the comedian love Halloween?

A: Because of all the joke-o'-lanterns!

Q: Why wasn't the computer allowed to drive?

A: Because it kept crashing!

Q: What's the most romantic thing about the ocean?

A: When the boats hug the shore!

Q: What goes "mooz-mooz"?

A: A race car going backward!

Q: Why is a riddle about a drill not funny?

A: It's bore-ing!

Q: How did the mermaid fall in love?

A: Head over eels!

Q: How do you get firewood?

A: Ax for it!

Q: What does the clothing store owner do before he goes on vacation?

A: He waters his pants!

Q: What kind of vehicle does a lumberjack drive?

A: A fir-by-fir!

Q: What do movie stars build their houses with?

A: Holly-wood!

Q: What did the television say to the remote control?

A: "Don't go changin'!"

Q: What is a golfer's favorite toy?

A: Silly putter!

Q: What is the laziest shoe?

A: A loafer!

Q: Why didn't the nose make the soccer team?

A: He didn't get picked!

Q: What did the ladder do on December 31?

A: He rung in the new year!

Q: What kind of ears do trains have?

A: Engine-ears!

Q: What do you do if you have a ring in your nose?

A: You better answer it!

Q: What nail is bad to hammer?

A: A fingernail!

Q: What's in the middle of the sun?

A: The letter *U*!

Q: What sport does a foot like to play?

A: Arch-ery!

Q: Why did the man get a bargain on his boat?

A: It was a sale boat!

Q: How do birds start their gym classes?

A: With worm-up exercises!

Q: What do you get when you cross the Flash with a toilet?

A: The Flush!

Q: What happens when a zombie is a chatterbox?

A: He will talk your ear off!

Q: Why was the refrigerator tired?

A: Because it had been running all day!

Q: What does a yo-yo do on vacation?

A: It unwinds!

Q: What's the difference between elephants and grapes?

A: Grapes are purple!

Q: What do you call Santa when he has a pocket full of change?

A: Saint Nickel-as!

Q: What do you get when you try to add 2 lorn plus 2 lorn?

A: For-lorn!

Q: What do you get when you cross a sprinter with a comedian?

A: A running joke!

Q: Why is Spider-Man often mistaken for a duck?

A: They both have webbed feet!

Q: What's black and yellow and goes "buzz-buzz"?

A: None of your bees-ness!

Q: Why did the millionaire take such good care of his pet?

A: Because it was a gold-fish!

Q: What finger do you use to turn to the end of a book?

A: The index finger!

Q: Can a rabbit jump higher than the Empire State Building?

A: Yes! The Empire State Building can't jump!

Q: What musical instrument do toothbrushes like to play?

A: A tuba toothpaste!

Q: What part of a car gets around the most?

A: The seat belt!

Q: What has an eye for sewing but can't see?

A: A needle!

Q: Where does the rabbit go to get her fur dyed?

A: To the hare dresser!

Q: Why couldn't the Human Torch get married?

A: He couldn't find his match!

Q: Why did the driver roll down his window?

A: Because he passed the gas station!

Q: What goes up but never comes down?

A: Your age!

Q: How did the letter *E* drown?

A: It found itself in the middle of the OCEAN!

Q: Why did the worm burrow into his computer?

A: It was an Apple!

Q: What do you call someone who repairs bicycles?

A: A spokes-person!

Q: Why do fleas always get so hungry between breakfast and dinner?

A: 'Cause there's no such thing as a flea lunch!

Q: How do you tell the weather on top of a mountain?

A: You climate!

Q: What does a lamp read?

A: Light reading!

Q: What do your pupils do in the winter?

A: They go eye-skating!

Q: What holds water even though it's full of holes?

A: A sponge!

Q: What do you call a talkative taxi driver?

A: A blabby cabby!

Q: What place honors firefighters?

A: The Hall of Flame!

Q: Why was the plant so smart?

A: It was a budding genius!

Q: What is a chicken's favorite vegetable?

A: Eggplant!

Q: What state can you write with?

A: Pencil-vania!

Q: What's the worst place to go on a picnic?

A: Ant-arctica!

Q: What kinds of bugs love the snow?

A: Mo-ski-toes!

Q: Where did the dog leave her car?

A: In the barking lot!

Q: Why did the hockey player go to orthodontist?

A: Because he had puck teeth!

Q: Where do comedians go when they're sick?

A: To the hee-hee-mergency room!

Q: Why was the gum so mad?

A: Because it got chewed out in class!

Q: What is a podiatrist's favorite channel?

A: The Foot Network!

Q: What did the snowstorm say to the mountain?

A: "Do you get my drift?"

Q: Why do underpants last so long?

A: Because they're never worn out!

Q: What is the longest word?

A: "Smiles"—there's a mile between the first and last letters!

Q: What is the best thing to put on your bed on a really hot day?

A: A sheet of ice!

Q: What do you get when you cross a mosquito and a computer?

A: A lot of bytes!

Q: Where is the best place to give your friend a high five?

A: Palm Beach!

Q: What kind of tree likes to visit the ocean?

A: A beech tree!

Q: Why was the broken piano locked out?

A: Because it didn't have any keys!

Q: Why does Batman use mouthwash?

A: To avoid bat breath!

Q: How does a wrestler keep his bike safe from thieves?

A: He puts it in a head-lock!

Q: Why was the computer called a hero?

A: Because he was always saving things!

Q: What is an astronaut's favorite day?

A: Moon-day!

Q: What kind of card do you send to a sheep?

A: A get wool card!

Q: Who likes to make dinner for Peter Pan?

A: Captain Cook!

Q: What kind of clothes do attorneys wear?

A: Law-suits!

Q: How does a sailor send computer messages?

A: Sea-mail!

Q: What did the tree get his girlfriend for her birthday?

A: A fir coat!

Q: What do you call a dog at the equator?

A: A hot dog!

Q: Why don't fish like hockey?

A: They're afraid of the net!

Q: Why was Cinderella thrown off the basketball team?

A: She ran away from the ball!

Q: What do you call a kiwi bird with no eyes?

A: A kw!

Q: What is the smelliest fish?

A: A stink ray!

Q: What kind of music do convicts like?

A: Rock and pa-role!

Q: **Why was the football player late for the game?**

A: He had to hike!

Q: **What do tennis players and butlers have in common?**

A: They both like to serve!

Q: **What did the nose say before he left?**

A: "I've got to run!"

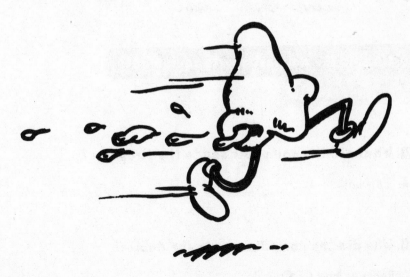

Q: What is the noisiest sports equipment?

A: A tennis racket!

Q: What did the computer say to the fireplace?

A: "Log on!"

Q: Why did the comedian go to the doctor?

A: Because he felt funny!

Q: Why did the campfire go to the doctor?

A: It had glowing pains!

Q: Where do you always find happiness?

A: In the dictionary!

Q: What school is the friendliest?

A: Hi school!

Q: Where do you buy a garage?

A: At a garage sale!

Q: What does Superman use to wake up in the morning?

A: An alarm Clark!

Q: Why did the computer graduate early?

A: Because he was upgraded!

Q: Why did the banana do well in gym class?

A: It could do splits!

Q: What did the raindrop say on his wedding day?

A: "I dew!"

Q: Which is the brainiest state?

A: Alabama. It has one *B* and four *A*'s!

Q: When the dish ran away with the spoon, where did they go?

A: China!

Q: What has four legs, antlers, and little red shorts?

A: Mickey Moose!

Q: With which finger should you dial the phone?

A: The ring finger!

Q: What color is the loudest?

A: Yell-ow!

Q: Why didn't people laugh at the scarecrow comedian?

A: Because he told corny jokes!

Q: What kind of music do cows like to listen to?

A: Moo-sic!

Q: Why did Thomas Edison have a good sense of humor?

A: He made light of everything!

Q: What do rainclouds wear?

A: Thunder-wear!

Q: Why is a garbage truck always depressed?

A: It's always down in the dumps!

Q: Why did the bachelor buy a calendar?

A: He wanted a lot of dates!

Q: Which is the richest body of water?

A: A river—it has two banks!

Q: What did one wall say to the other wall?

A: "I'll meet you at the corner!"

Q: What did the artist try to do when he got in trouble?

A: Take the easel way out!

Q: How did the rubber band get to the airport?

A: In a s-t-r-e-t-c-h limo!

Q: What does an astronaut carry a sandwich in?

A: A launch box!

Q: Why do kids have to go to bed?

A: Because their beds won't come to them!

Q: What has four wheels and flies?

A: A garbage truck!

Q: What goes across the country but stays in a corner?

A: A stamp!

Q: Why are fish so smart?

A: Because they swim in schools!

Q: How many sides does a sphere have?

A: Two! An inside and an outside!

Q: Why did the ladder fail his driver's exam?

A: He made all the rung turns!

Q: Why was the computer held back a grade?

A: Because he couldn't get his fax right!

Q: Why did the acrobat quit his job?

A: It was making him flip out!

Q: What does a riddle writer use to cook?

A: A frying pun!

Q: What kind of flowers did the rope send to the string?

A: Forget-me-knots!

Q: What do you say to someone when they try to take your cheese?

A: "That's nacho cheese!"

Q: What kind of driver never gets anywhere?

A: A screwdriver!

Q: How do bees greet one another?

A: With a hive five!

Q: What did the log say to the ashes?

A: "You're fired!"

Q: What do you call a telephone placed next to a window?

A: A sill phone!

Q: Why did the baseball player get arrested?

A: She stole a base!

Q: What runs along a yard without moving?

A: A fence!

Q: Where do sheep get their hair cut?

A: At the baa-baa shop!

Q: Why did the girl ride the camel?

A: Because it was too heavy to carry!

Q: Why did the cookie call in sick?

A: She was feeling crumb-y!

Q: Why was the mailbox fat?

A: Because it ate too much junk mail!

Q: How do you know that a clock is hungry?

A: It goes back for seconds!

Q: What did the reflection say to the doctor?

A: "I don't feel like myself!"

Q: Why was the weatherman so scared?

A: Because he was terrified of Fahren-heights!

Q: Where did the zookeeper sign his new contract?

A: On the dotted lion!

Q: What do you call a snowstorm in Oz?

A: The Blizzard of Oz!

Q: Why is six afraid of seven?

A: Because seven ate nine!

Q: What did the sleepy king say to the brave dragon slayer?

A: "Good knight!"

Q: What city wanders around aimlessly?

A: Rome!

Q: What city has the best eyesight?

A: See-atle!

Q: What did the tree say on the first day of spring?

A: "I'm turning over a new leaf!"

Q: What did the policeman say to the noisy motorist?

A: "Look before you beep!"

Q: What makes more noise than a baby getting a new tooth?

A: Two babies getting new teeth!

Q: What did the square say to the circle?

A: "Meet me at the corner!"

Q: If April showers bring May flowers, what do May flowers bring?

A: Pilgrims!

Q: What do you call a train that puts money under your pillow?

A: The toot fairy!

Q: Why was Cinderella a bad soccer player?

A: She had a pumpkin for a coach!

Q: Where do aliens place their teacups?

A: On flying saucers!

Q: What city has the most rowboats?

A: Oar-lando!

Q: What do skaters shave with?

A: Roller-blades!

Q: When are bowling balls the saddest?

A: When they end up in the gutter!

Q: What kind of books does a race-car driver like to read?

A: Auto-biographies!

Q: When does a house know something is wrong?

A: When it gets a lot of stairs!

Q: What flower does everyone have?

A: Everyone has two-lips!

Q: What is a skeleton's favorite food?

A: Spare ribs!

Q: Why was the musician sad?

A: He couldn't compose himself!

Q: What's a polygon?

A: A parrot that escaped from its cage!

Q: What city is tilted?

A: New Or-leans!

Q: How does lettuce get around town?

A: In a horse-drawn cabbage!

Q: Why did the mechanic tear apart his computer?

A: He was looking for the search engine!

Q: How do you get down from a mule?

A: You don't get down from a mule, you get down from a goose!

Q: What did one shoe say to the other shoe?

A: "Your lace is familiar!"

Q: How did the toupee get started in the movies?

A: He got a small part!

Q: What has only one hand?

A: An arm!

Q: What flower is a candy?

A: A lolli-poppy!

Q: What type of music do you hear in a cave?

A: Rock!

Q: Where is lunch served to football players?

A: The Soup Bowl!

Q: What does a bat need in order to run?

A: A bat-tery!

Q: What is a zombie's favorite dessert?

A: Ice scream!

Q: What has legs but can't walk?

A: A table!

Q: What is a runner's favorite part of a car?

A: The dash-board!

Q: What kind of jeans ring?

A: Bell bottoms!

Q: What tool goes up and down?

A: A see-saw!

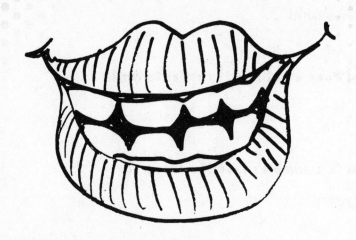

Q: When is a mouth the happiest?

A: During lip year!

Q: Which country's capital is having a population expansion?

A: Dublin, Ireland!

Q: What did the Pilgrims have to clean after the first Thanksgiving dinner?

A: The Mess-achusetts!

Q: What did the red rose say to the pink rose?

A: "What's up, bud?"

Q: What's the sleepiest thing at the dinner table?

A: The nap-kins!

Q: Why wasn't Batman able to catch any fish?

A: Robin ate all the worms!

Q: What city lends out a lot of money?

A: Barce-loan-a!

Q: Why did the broom take a nap?

A: He was sweep-y!

Q: How many farts does it take to fill an auditorium?

A: Quite a phew!

Q: What smells the best at dinnertime?

A: Your nose!

Q: Why do you want the rain to keep up?

A: Because then it won't come down!

Q: Where do you keep a taxi?

A: In a cab-inet!

Q: Why did the jogger go to the doctor?

A: He was feeling run down!

Q: Where does Santa keep all his red suits?

A: In the Claus-et!

Q: What did the guitar say to the guitar player?

A: "Stop picking on me!"

Q: Where do glasses like to go on Saturday nights?

A: To the eye-ball!

Q: What did one telephone give the other on Valentine's Day?

A: A ring!

Q: Why was Plymouth Rock so brave?

A: Because he was a little bold-er!

Q: What do construction workers use to block traffic in winter?

A: Snow cones!

Q: How do you make the number seven even?

A: Take away the *S*!

Q: What did the artist say at the start of the duel?

A: "Draw!"

Q: What do you call it when a martial arts expert gets sick?

A: Kung flu!

Q: What did Obi-Wan say to Luke Skywalker while having lunch?

A: "May the fork be with you!"

Q: What always comes at the end of a road?

A: The letter *D*!

Q: What winter sport do trees participate in?

A: Al-pine skiing!

Q: Why did the tongue stay up late?

A: Because he was cramming for a taste test!

Q: How did the basketball court get wet?

A: The players dribbled all over it!

Q: What is sawdust?

A: The past tense of see dust!

Q: What part of the body is most like a tree?

A: Your palm!

Q: Why did the waiter always win at tennis?

A: He had the best serve!

Q: What did the shoe say to the piece of gum?

A: "Stick with me and we'll go places!"

Q: How does a pilot get from one floor to another?

A: He takes a flight of stairs!

Q: Why did the window go to the doctor?

A: It had a pane!

Q: What did the robber say to the Post-it note?

A: "Stick 'em up!"

Q: What dance do arms and legs like the most?

A: The limb-o!

Q: Where does Wednesday come after Thursday?

A: In the dictionary!

Q: What is slimy and grants wishes?

A: The Wizard of Ooze!

Q: Why was the computer in the freezer?

A: It was frozen!

Q: What is something you never want to see on a cruise ship?

A: A sink!

Q: What did the big bucket say to the little bucket?

A: "You look a little pail!"

Craig Yoe has been an award-winning creative director for Disney, Nickelodeon, and the Muppets and looks funny.